REJECTION IS HELL!

Freedom from the pain

by

JONAS CLARK

A SPIRIT OF LIFE CLASSIC

Unless otherwise indicated, all Scripture quotations are taken from the *King James Version* of the Bible.

REJECTION IS HELL!
Freedom from the pain
ISBN 1-886885-16-8

Published by Spirit of Life Publishing
27 West Hallandale Beach Blvd.
Hallandale, Florida
33009-5437, U.S.A.
(954) 456-4420

01 02 03 04 05 06 07 ♦ 07 06 05 04 03 02 01

ABOUT
THE AUTHOR

The anointing on his life is both bold and strong. Jonas' great passion is to take this gospel of the kingdom into all the world. Fortitude and God's grace have taken the ministry international, carrying a message of divine impact and reform for this generation into over twenty-three nations. Jonas is...

pioneer of the Global Cause Network (GCN), a fellowship of over 58 churches around the world of like precious faith.

senior editor of The Ambassador Journal (www.catchlife.org), an internet magazine and prophetic journal sent to thousands of leaders in more than 62 countries, the New Apostolic Voice for the 21st Century.

a prolific writer who has authored many books with an apostolic and prophetic voice that are catching the attention of the church.

founder of Spirit of Life Publishing which provides critical learning resources, educational and informational materials throughout the nations.

pioneer of The Harvest Strategy, a reforming ministry structure for city-wide evangelism.

founder of Spirit of Life Ministries in Hallandale Beach, Florida, an apostolic training center.

As a reformer, his desire is to see the nations of the world impacted and changed by the power of God. Jonas has been in the ministry for seventeen years. He is blessed with his beautiful wife Rhonda and three daughters Natasha, Nichole and Natalie.

Dedicated to Nichole

"On the mount of great horses
sit those with God's courage.
Stand fast young champion,
the greatest race is still ahead
-- your life."

Love Dad

Once I looked for a cloud in the sky. The harder I looked the higher it seemed. Then one day I didn't look anymore. To my surprise it wasn't there.

What have you stopped looking for?

by Jonas Clark

CONTENTS

FOREWORD

In the apostolic move that we see arising today, I am seeing a new breed of ministers beginning to come forth. These ministers are completely sold out to the cause of Christ; men and women who lay down their lives to see the Gospel of Christ preached throughout the world. These ministers deny themselves in order to see the body of Christ set free and members of the body step into the fullness of their call. One of these modern apostles is Jonas Clark. Apostle Clark has been ministering to the body of Christ for eighteen years, fulfilling his call as an apostle to the nations. From the day that I first met him, he has greatly influenced my life by challenging me, prompting me, and stretching me. With his encouragement, I have done things I would never have attempted on my own.

In my twenty years of ministry, I have found a common denominator in the lives

1

of those who fight insecurity, inferiority, and depression. That common denominator is rejection. In *Rejection is Hell*, Apostle Clark exposes the tool of rejection that the enemy has used against the Church. Jonas draws from his many years of experience in ministering to hurting people. His transparency in sharing his own battles with rejection reminds us that we all have pain and that Jesus has come to heal our broken hearts.

One of the most powerful aspects of this book is the way in which the Holy Spirit took Jonas behind the scenes in the lives of many of the great men and women in the Bible who experienced failure because they failed to recognize and deal with the rejection in their lives. Rejection is one of the tools in Satan's arsenal that causes us to be unable to function in the church. There are many wonderful, gifted and anointed members of the Body of Christ whose gifts and ministries have been neutralized by rejection. Let's learn from the mistakes of those mentioned in this book so that we don't fall into the same traps and miss our rewards.

I am convinced that after reading this book, each reader will be able to locate the root of the pain in their lives and will be able to receive the healing provided for in the Atonement of Jesus Christ. It is often said, "Hurting people hurt people." If the church is to stop hurting one another, the pain must first be stopped in each of us. The pain we hold causes walls to be built between our family, friends, our God, and us. This book is definitely a key to the healing that the Body of Christ must experience in order to work together in taking the Gospel of Christ to the world.

Jonas Clark has written this book under the unction of the Holy Spirit. As you read it, let that anointing minister to you and destroy the yokes of bondage that have kept you from fulfilling your call.

Thank you, Jonas, for being a vessel that God can use to bring healing to His Body.

David Coker
Faith Christian Fellowship
Carnesville, Georgia

INTRODUCTION

The pain of rejection is one of the most horrible things a person can deal with. The torment is almost unbearable and impossible to describe.

When I was a little boy, I lived in a home with parents that fought and abused each other continually. One day my only sister, who was four years old, drowned in the canal behind our house. Even though I was only six years old at the time, I distinctly remember my mother's desperate cries for help when talking to the telephone operator. I remember the paramedic's frantic efforts to revive my sister without success. The grief in my house was unbelievable. From that day forward the climate in our home was worse than ever. My mother blamed my father, who in turn blamed her for the death of my beautiful sister. Somehow I felt that I, too, was to blame. The pain of that tragic day was too much for them to bear, so my parents separated when I was only nine years old.

5

When my father left I felt abandoned. Why did he leave us? What had I done wrong? That day put a pain of rejection in my heart that affected me for many years. Like many of you I discovered that 'rejection is hell.'

If you are struggling with rejection, my prayer is that you will experience the same healing, freedom and love of Jesus that I did. He will give you a peace that will not go away.

From South Florida,
Jonas Clark

CHAPTER 1

THE HOUSE
THAT REJECTION BUILT

Rejection is one of the most prevalent hindrances of spiritual maturity in the body of Christ today. It is amazing to see how many people respond to life through hurts, wounds, pains, and scars from the past. As you read the following pages, my prayer is that you may be able to understand the root of rejection, and how to achieve freedom from its intolerable assignment.

I will spend some time pulling apart the different elements of rejection so that all can understand why we feel and act the way we do. Throughout, I will refer to rejection as a personality malfunction, and a house that has been built by using the

7

wrong construction materials. We will also review the various ways that God's people dealt with rejection throughout the scriptures. From looking at the lives of others, we can learn to modify our own behavior and become all that God wants us to be. With that said, let's go right to the heart of the matter -- rejection is hell.

Through the years I have met thousands that suffered from rejection. It is astounding to see just how many people are affected in some manner by this malady. But what exactly is rejection?

Rejection is the feeling of not being liked, accepted, loved, valued, or received.

It is the state of feeling unwanted, unaccepted, or unappreciated. Those with rejection personalities internalize their feelings, which create, over the years, a false personality. This false personality is 'the house that rejection built.' These feelings are such things as...

feelings of worthlessness.

wishing you had never been born.

feelings of inferiority.

guilt.

PERSONALITY MALFUNCTION

The 'rejected' measure their self-worth based upon acceptance. When not accepted, they devalue their self-worth, which negatively affects their personalities. So then *rejection* creates a personality malfunction caused by...

hurts

wounds

pain

generational curses

divorce

betrayal

trauma

abandonment

neglect

violated trust

handicaps

abuse.

REJECTION'S
CONSTRUCTION MATERIALS

Whether the hurt and pain be real or perceived is irrelevant to those suffering from rejection. The root cause of a rejection personality malfunction is pain. Satan takes advantage of our pain and uses it to launch us into building a house using rejection's building materials. Typically, a person with rejection's personality has spent years building a house (personality) made of construction materials that are not from God. Those *construction materials* are such things as...

a melancholy outlook on life.

fear of people's opinion of you.

always trying to fit in but never really feeling that you belong.

thinking that good things belong to everyone but you.

seeking the attention and approval of others, etc.

Through prayer and deliverance we can bring about healing, but the false personality that was built by rejection must be torn down bit by bit and rebuilt by submitting and conforming ourselves to the word of God. We must be taught how to separate feelings from truth.

Rejection wants to tell you who you are and give you value and self-esteem through works rather than an identity provided by Christ. Because of a 'works' attempt to achieve self-worth, they will either become introverted and do nothing at all, because "after all, what's the use?" Or, they become extraverted and use work to validate their worth and prove themselves to others. We must learn to identify the stimuli that trigger feelings of rejection, understand the sources of the sensitivity, and submit them to the truth of God's word.

SUMMARY
THE HOUSE
THAT REJECTION BUILT

Rejection is the feeling of not being liked, accepted, loved, valued, or received.

Those with rejection personalities internalize their feelings of rejection, which create, over the years, a false personality.

The root cause of a rejection personality malfunction is pain.

Rejection creates a personality disorder caused by hurts, wounds, pain, generational curses, divorce, trauma, abandonment, neglect, or abuse.

Through prayer and deliverance we can bring about healing, but the false personality built by rejection must be torn down bit by bit and rebuilt by submitting and conforming ourselves to the word of God.

Rejection wants to tell you who you are, give you value and self-esteem through works rather than an identity provided by Christ.

CHAPTER 2

THIS OLD HOUSE

Rejection wants to give you an identity. It is a force that will try to conform, mold, and impart to you a wrong personality. *The rejected personality is not the real you.* We can't let the hurt of yesterday determine our identity today. You are who God says you are.

Renewing our minds with the word of God is the first major step toward freedom with those who suffer from rejection. If we do not think right, then we cannot believe right. If we do not believe right, then we will never be able to act right.

It is important to understand that we cannot trust our soulish nature to tell us who we are. Within the building that rejection built is inner agony and a great struggle to be accepted. However, past experiences will always taint and falsely color the way we see ourselves and the way we respond to those around us.

RENOVATING THE OLD HOUSE

To free ourselves from the past we must renovate our minds with truth. Our rejected experiences have built a house according to the blueprints of pain and hurt. 'This old house' must be torn down and built again. Freedom from rejection comes partly from the success of your renovation project. To renew means to renovate. Let's take a look.

> "And be not conformed to this world: but be ye transformed by the renewing (renovation) of your mind, that ye may prove what is that good, and accept-able, and perfect, will of God." (Romans 12:2 KJV)

The word *transformed* is the Greek word *metamorphoo* meaning to be changed into another form. This teaches us that the word of God, when used to renovate our minds, will gradually morph us into the proper personality.

Notice that the above scripture deals with the mind of man and not the spirit of man.

When you repented of your sins and asked Jesus for forgiveness, you became a new creature in Christ Jesus, "Old things are passed away; behold, all things are become new" (2 Corinthians 5:17). However, that dealt with your spirit man, the real you. But your soul man still had issues that needed to be dealt with.

The *soul of man* is the mind, will, intellect, reasoning, imaginations and emotions. All of these must come into conformity to the will of God through submission to the word of God. Only then can our personalities be morphed into our proper identities.

We must not look at the word of God's ability to renovate our minds as a trivial thing. If we reject the knowledge of God, we will continue to allow the pain of rejection to tell us who we are. Applied knowledge of the word of God is the key to the success of our renovation project.

> "My people are destroyed for lack of knowledge: because thou hast rejected knowledge, I will also reject (*ma'ac*) thee..." (Hosea 4:6 KJV).

REJECTING KNOWLEDGE

Rejection of knowledge (God's word) gives rejection the right to continue to operate.

The word teaches us that if we are "hearers only" and not "doers of the word" of God, then we "deceive ourselves" and continue to walk in the rejected personality. The applied word of God is our key to victory!

> "But be ye doers of the word, and not hearers only, *deceiving your own selves.* {23} For if any be a hearer of the word, and not a doer, he is like unto a man beholding his natural face in a glass: {24} For he beholdeth himself, and goeth his way, and straightway forgetteth what manner (sort) of man he was. {25} But whoso looketh into the perfect law of liberty, and continueth therein, he being not a forgetful hearer, but a doer of the work, this man shall be blessed in his deed." (James 1:22-25 KJV Italics added)

To *deceive* is the Greek word *paralogizomai* meaning to...

reckon wrongly.

cheat yourself.

have a false reasoning.

delude.

circumvent.

Deception is a condition caused by refusing to walk out (obey) the word of God. It is impossible to renovate our minds with truth if we do not obey the truth. Renovation is a *process* of tearing down the learned behavior that rejection built. The truth we obey is the truth that will tear down the rejected personality. In the next chapter, we will begin to examine the causes of rejection.

SUMMARY
THIS OLD HOUSE

The rejected personality is not the real you.

Rejection wants to give you an identity.

Within the building that rejection built is inner agony and a great struggle to be accepted.

Past experiences will always taint and falsely color the way we see ourselves and respond to those around us.

Renewing our minds with the word of God is the first major step toward freedom with those who suffer from rejection.

Freedom from rejection comes partly from the success of your renovation project.

The word *transformed* is the Greek word *metamorphoo* meaning to be changed into another form.

The soul of man is the mind, will, intellect, reasoning, imaginations and emotions. All of these must come into conformity to the will of God through submission to the word of God.

Applied knowledge of the word of God is the key to our renovation project.

The truth we obey is the truth that will tear down the rejected personality.

CHAPTER 3

TRAITS OF REJECTION

Everyone has to face rejection because it is a part of everyday life. We cannot avoid rejection because we cannot control the way people feel about us. However ,we can control our response. Some will like us automatically; others may reject us without reason. People are turned down every day for pay raises, refused job promotions, declined for loans, taken for granted, treated poorly, and passed over for due recognition. All of these are real life situations. So why do some face more difficulty than others? Could it have more to do with feelings? Is rejection an emotional response or an objective response to life? Does rejection push a button that causes some sort of internalization and diminishing of self-worth? As we continue along in our study, let's explore the possibility that the negative feelings caused by rejection are because of an improper internalization of various events.

CAUSES OF REJECTION

Rejection is the feeling (internalization) that we are not being valued or accepted. For example, each of us has the basic need to feel accepted. When we do not feel accepted, then we must learn how to deal with the negative feelings of that rejection. We cannot depend on being accepted by others to give us our sense of self-worth. Before we can get free from the causes of rejection, we must try to pinpoint the source of the feelings. This is what I call rejection's trigger. That trigger mechanism must be dismantled. The causes for rejection are as diverse as there are people. *Causes of rejection* can stem from...

a lack of love from a spouse, parent, or grandparent.

an unwanted pregnancy.

the trauma of divorce.

the abandonment by a friend
or loved one.

a violation of trust.

abuse whether physically, emotionally, or sexually.

public humiliation.

a failure.

a bankruptcy.

poor performance academically
or in sports.

Some indicators of rejection are included
in the following list of questions. Do you
have problems with any of them? Take your
time as you prayerfully read the list, and let
the Holy Spirit begin to speak to your heart.
Now is the time to be completely honest with
yourself. You are reading this book because
you are trying to understand rejection.
Answering these questions truthfully will
help you learn more about yourself and how
to minister to others. As you read the
questions, put a check mark beside those
things that seem to trouble you.

__ Do you have a fear of people's opinion of

__ Do you have a fear of people's opinion of you?

__ Are you a perfectionist?

__ Are you frustrated with life?

__ Are you abnormally anxious?

__ Do you project a false sense of superiority?

__ Are you suspicious of anything nice done for you?

__ Do you have difficulty trusting God and others?

__ Do you have difficulty understanding the love of God?

__ Do you have difficulty demonstrating love to others?

__ Do you think that God cannot use you?

__ Do you ask yourself, "How can God love me?"

__ To "feel special" will you do extreme things like dangerous sports?

__ Do you have severe bouts with depression and thoughts of suicide?

__ Do you hide behind pets, books, hobbies, or work?

__ Do you over emphasize material possessions? What about in dress or appearance?

__ Do you have a domineering air or way about you?

__ Do you have a critical spirit?

__ Have you entered a self-imposed isolation from others?

__ Do you feel empty and unfulfilled?

__ Do you have a difficult time receiving love?

__ Are there times when you don't want anyone to touch you?

__ Do you value acceptance and hate correction?

__ Do you have feelings of inferiority?

__ Do you think that God does not love you as much as others?

__ Do you dress for attention?

__ Do you have a fear to communicate your opinions?

__ Do you detest being compared to others?

__ Do you have uncontrolled bouts with pent up anger?

__ Are there times when you feel undeserving?

__ Do you feel that your lot in life is to suffer?

__ Do you have a fear of failure?

__ Are you a workaholic or overachiever?

__ Do you take things way too personally?

__ Would you rather spend your time with pets than people?

__ Do you have a woe-is-me, melancholy view of life?

__ Are you afraid to tell the truth about your feelings?

__ Do you constantly fight discouragement?

__ Are you harshly judgmental of others?

__ Are you a faultfinder?

__ Are you afraid of God?

__ Are you always on the defensive?

__ Do you have a problem relating to the opposite sex?

__ Are you a procrastinator?

__ Do you feel stupid, inferior, or self-conscious when around other people?

__ Do you resent and hold bitterness toward others?

__ Do you feel like you need to seek attention from others?

__ Do you feel like you can never measure up to others?

__ Are you driven to prove yourself to others?

__ Are you troubled with constant mind traffic that gives you no rest?

__ Do you have a problem saying, 'No' when you know that you need to?

__ Do you feel threatened by others?

__ Do you attack those you love and don't understand why?

__ Do you think that no one really understands you?

__ Are you drawn towards base people who seem to be more accepting yet do nothing to bring stability in your life?

__ Are you sometimes very introverted and at other times very extraverted?

__ Do you avoid being involved in group activities?

__ Do you try to fit in with the crowd but never really feel that you belong?

The checklist above is provided only to stir your thinking and allow the Holy Spirit to begin to reveal some of the root causes of why you feel the way you do. Once we recognize rejection, then we can begin the healing and rebuilding process. If you checked several of the items on the list, perhaps you are having difficulty with rejection. Don't worry – I have great news for you. Jesus is the answer to all of our problems. He understands you better than you understand yourself. He has offered us a way of escape. His word will teach you what to do. There is hope for you! In the next chapter, we will learn how Samuel handled rejection.

SUMMARY
TRAITS OF REJECTION

Everyone will face rejection because it is a part of everyday life.

We cannot avoid rejection because we cannot control the way people feel about us.

The negative feelings caused by rejection are an improper internalization of various events.

Rejection is the feeling (*internalization*) that we are not being valued or accepted.

When we do not feel accepted we must learn how to deal with the negative feelings of that rejection.

We cannot depend on being
accepted by others to give us
our sense of self-worth.

CHAPTER 4

MINISTERIAL REJECTION

Everyone in the ministry has had to face rejection. I remember the negative feelings that bombarded my mind the first time someone got up and walked out of a service when I was preaching. It was a painful experience and forced me to deal with the spirit of rejection. The gospel of Jesus Christ is the most accepted and rejected message in history. Every minister of the gospel must quickly learn that it is not they but Christ who is being rejected. The prophet Samuel faced strong feelings of rejection. Let's look at his ministry and how he overcame those feelings.

The first mention of Samuel is found when his mother Hannah promised God that if He would grant her a son she would

29

give that son back to Him as a Nazarite (1 Samuel 1:11). Soon after her vow Hannah conceived a child and named him Samuel. After weaning Samuel, Hannah, along with her husband Elkanah, delivered the young child to Shilo where Samuel was left in the care of Eli the high priest. Thereafter Hannah and Elkanah visited their son Samuel only once each year (1 Samuel 2:19). Samuel never returned to his home in Ramah as a child. Sometimes I wonder if Samuel felt the least bit rejected when his parents left him with Eli. We may never know. Nevertheless, years later we find Samuel facing feelings of rejection in his ministry. Let's take a look.

God spoke to Samuel about the rejection he was feeling when he was displeased with the people because they asked for a king to govern them like all the heathen nations around them. Samuel took those feelings of rejection to the Lord in prayer. The Lord answered Samuel, "Hearken unto the voice of the people in all that they say unto thee: for they have not rejected (*ma'ac*) thee, but they have rejected me, that I should not reign over them" (1 Samuel 8:7 KJV).

Like many of us, Samuel felt that the people of God had rejected him when they turned away from the counsel of God. Those in the ministry constantly face this type of rejection. When hit with feelings of rejection it is important not to internalize those feelings. To *internalize* means to take the rejection personally by making it your own.

Samuel's response to the feelings of rejection from the people was to take it to God in prayer. Scripture declares, "Casting all your care upon him; for he careth for you" (1 Peter 5:7).

Responding to Samuel's prayer, the Lord pointed to the root of those feelings of rejection by letting the prophet know that because of the people's rebellion they were rejecting him.

Oftentimes people who are prophetic face a titanic battle with rejection. Prophets are the most spiritually sensitive of all the five-fold ascension gifts, but they must understand that it is the Lord himself who is being rejected and not them. It was the rebellion against God's authority and His divine right to rule (govern) the people that was the instrument for a release of the spirit of rejection against Samuel.

ABANDONMENT AND REJECTION

The people's rejection of God also caused them to abandon Samuel. Rejection and abandonment travel together. The Lord declared, "I brought them up out of Egypt even unto this day, wherewith they have forsaken me, and served other gods, so do they also unto thee" (1 Samuel 8:8). The word *forsaken* is the Hebrew word *azab* meaning to...

depart

leave

desert

forsake

neglect

abandon.

Those who operate out of rejection will forsake and abandon those who love them the most. God told Samuel to tell the people, who chose to abandon and reject him for another, what life would be like for them when they had a king.

"And he said, This will be the manner of the king that shall reign over you: He will take your sons, and appoint them for himself, for his chariots, and to be his horsemen; and some shall run before his chariots. {12} And he will appoint him captains over thousands, and captains over fifties; and will set them to ear his ground, and to reap his harvest, and to make his instruments of war, and instruments of his chariots. {13} And he will take your daughters to be confectionaries, and to be cooks, and to be bakers. {14} And he will take your fields, and your vineyards, and your oliveyards, even the best of them, and give them to his servants. {15} And he will take the tenth of your seed, and of your vineyards, and give to his officers, and to his servants. {16} And he will take your menservants, and your maidservants, and your goodliest young men, and your asses, and put them to his work. {17} He will take the tenth of your sheep: and ye shall be his servants." (1 Samuel 8:11-17 KJV)

From the above scriptures we discover that a person with rejection who refuses to submit to the rule of God will lose the liberty that he takes for granted and exchange it for the control and lordship of another.

ACCEPTANCE
FROM THE WRONG PEOPLE

It is very common to see someone with the spirit of rejection not appreciate those who love them. Nor do they recognize the graciousness of their true friends and sincere relatives. I have seen them reject their godly friends only to be controlled and dominated by self-serving manipulators such as Jezebel, Ahab, and Balaam. The Lord emphasizes over and over that the new king "will take." *To take (laqach)* means to...

lay-hold of

seize

carry away

procure to himself

capture

remove.

Sadly, even after Samuel pleaded with the people to reconsider their request they "refused to obey the voice of Samuel." They rejected him because they wanted a king over them "like all the nations" (1 Samuel 8:19). *Samuel handled the rejection properly*

by not taking their rejection personally.
Samuel did not internalize his feelings. The
truth that helped Samuel press through the
rejection was in understanding that the
people were rejecting God and not him.
When you have the approval of God, man's
opinion or your feelings are irrelevant.

Just as Israel wanted a king so that they
could be like the other nations, those with
rejection also want to *feel accepted* by the
wrong people. The people of Israel no longer
wanted to depend on God's word nor a life
of faith. They exchanged their all sufficient
King for another. In the next chapter we
will look at the rejection that David faced
and how he overcame it.

SUMMARY
MINISTERIAL REJECTION

Samuel felt the people were
rejecting him but in reality
they were rejecting God.

When hit with feelings of
rejection it is important not to
internalize those feelings. To
internalize means to take the
rejection personally and make
it your own.

The instrument for the spirit of rejection is refusal to submit to the rule (government) of the Lord Jesus Christ and his word.

Those who operate out of rejection will forsake and abandon those who love them the most.

The person with rejection who refuses to submit to the rule of God will lose the liberty that he takes for granted and *exchange* it for the control and lordship of another.

Those with rejection do not appreciate those who love them.

Those with rejection want to *feel* accepted by the wrong people.

CHAPTER 5

A FATHER'S REJECTION

If there is anyone in the word of God that must have understood rejection surely it was King David. Of all those written about in the word of God, I think that David is one of the most fascinating and inspiring. There are so many aspects of his life and faith that we can all relate to on a personal level. Even though he seemed to be this stalwart man of steel and strength he was also sensitive and tender. David is most remembered as the young lad who slew Goliath and became the Champion of Israel. As we study his testimony, however, we discover that his family life was far from perfect. As a matter of fact, his family life was a mess. It was totally dysfunctional.

Many times throughout David's life he

faced rejection's strong pillars but managed to find strength in God to overcome. In spite of David's flaws, we can learn from this man who "was after God's own heart" (Acts 13:22). His life was such an encouragement to those who suffer the pains of rejection.

In this chapter, we are going to look at the times when David was rejected and how he overcame. David was rejected by...

his natural father, Jesse.

his brothers.

King Saul, his spiritual father.

his wife Michal.

his close friend.

his son Absalom.

The first mention of David is when Samuel was sent by God to anoint for himself a king. We find Samuel the prophet being sent to Jesse the Bethlehemite to anoint one of his sons to become that sought after king. Let's take a look.

> "And the LORD said unto Samuel, How long wilt thou mourn for Saul, seeing I have

> rejected him from reigning over
> Israel? fill thine horn with oil,
> and go, I will send thee to Jesse
> the Bethlehemite: for I have
> provided me a king among his
> sons." (1 Samuel 16:1)

After arriving at Bethlehem, Samuel invited Jesse to attend a very special sacrifice to the Lord and to bring along his sons. Samuel didn't tell Jesse that he had been sent by the Lord to anoint a king yet it must have been quite an honor for Jesse's family to be personally invited to this gathering. Samuel must have been really impressed when he looked at Jesse's seven fine looking sons. They were good looking, tall and strong. Surely the Lord's Anointed was among them. There was Eliab, Abinadab, Shammah, and four others who stood before the prophet of God. Let's take a look at the scriptures that describe this meeting.

> Samuel said to Jesse, "I am
> come to sacrifice unto the
> LORD: sanctify yourselves, and
> come with me to the sacrifice.
> And he sanctified Jesse and his
> sons, and called them to the
> sacrifice. {6} And it came to pass,
> when they were come, that he

looked on Eliab, and said,
Surely the Lord's anointed is
before him. {7} But the LORD
said unto Samuel, Look not on
his countenance, or on the
height of his stature; because I
have refused him: for the
LORD seeth not as man seeth;
for man looketh on the outward
appearance, but the LORD
looketh on the heart. {8} Then
Jesse called Abinadab, and
made him pass before Samuel.
And he said, Neither hath the
LORD chosen this. {9} Then
Jesse made Shammah to pass
by. And he said, Neither hath
the LORD chosen this. {10}
Again, Jesse made seven of his
sons to pass before Samuel.
And Samuel said unto Jesse,
The LORD hath not chosen
these." (1 Samuel 16:5-10 KJV)

Samuel was ready to fulfill his mission
but the Lord had chosen none of those sons.
Samuel surely was perplexed, but God told
him that he "looketh on the heart" and not
on the outward appearance. Samuel then
asked Jesse if he had any more children.

"And Samuel said unto Jesse,
Are here all thy children? And
he said, There remaineth yet
the youngest, and, behold, he
keepeth the sheep. And
Samuel said unto Jesse, Send
and fetch him: for we will not
sit down till he come hither.
{12} And he sent, and brought
him in. Now he was ruddy, and
withal of a beautiful countenance, and goodly to look to.
And the LORD said, Arise,
anoint him: for this is he. {13}
Then Samuel took the horn of
oil, and anointed him in the
midst of his brethren: and the
spirit of the LORD came upon
David from that day forward. So
Samuel rose up, and went to
Ramah." (1 Samuel 16:11-13
KJV)

I think that it is very interesting that
Jesse did not have David meet with the
prophet along with his other sons. It would
have been a simple matter to have someone
else tend the sheep for that special
occasion. After all, how often did a prophet
come to town and invite the entire family to
a special service?

Samuel was insistent that Jesse call his

missing son, and he waited for the youngest to arrive. As soon as Samuel saw David,
the Lord spoke saying, "Arise and anoint
him in the midst of his brethren." David
was God's chosen vessel. Although the
other family members did not recognize the
value of this young lad, God truly did. Then
the "Spirit of the Lord came on David from
that day forward."

These events cause us to ask some
important questions. Why didn't Jesse
include David in the meeting? Could it be
that he didn't consider him important
enough to meet with the prophet? What was
David's relationship with his older brothers?
What about his father? Where was David's
mother? Had she died giving birth to David?
Was David received by his brothers or was
he rejected by them?

After the Lord refused to anoint David's
brothers, did this cause them to feel
rejected? Regardless of your conclusion, the
important thing to notice is that God looks
on the heart of man when he makes his
decision to anoint someone. It is also
important to note that one must keep his
heart right before the Lord regardless of
everyone else's opinion of his value.

From this, we learn that everyone is
important to the Lord. Even when it appears
that you have been rejected or left out by a
parent, God has not left you out. In fact,

our Lord will do whatever it takes to reach you. Our God has not rejected us but has received us. He does not look on the outward appearance as man looks but looks at our heart. Great is our God!

SUMMARY
A FATHER'S REJECTION

His father, brothers, King Saul, wife, close friend, and his son Absalom all rejected David.

Jesse did not have David at the meeting with Samuel along with his other sons.

God looks on the heart of man when he makes his decision to anoint someone.

Even when it appears that you have been rejected or left out by a parent, God has not left you out.

CHAPTER 6

SIBLING REJECTION

Sibling rivalry exists to some extent between all siblings. However, there are many times when sibling rivalry turns into abuse and sets children up to deal with issues of rejection in their life. Let's take a look at David's relationship with his brothers.

One day the Philistines gathered their armies to battle against Israel. The Philistines stood on a mountain on one side and Israel stood on a mountain on the other side. There was only a valley between the two armies. The Philistines presented their champion warrior named Goliath of Gath whose height was six cubits and a span. As Goliath approached the armies of Israel he mocked and challenged them. He could be heard throughout all the camp of Israel taunting, "Why did you come out to set your battle in array? Am not I a Philistine, and you servants to Saul? Choose you a man for you, and let him come down to me. {9} If he be able to fight with me, and to kill me, then will we be your servants: but if I prevail against him, and kill him, then shall ye be our servants, and serve us." If that was not serious enough then he said, "I defy the armies of Israel this day; give me a man that we may fight together" (1 Samuel 17:8-10).

Goliath was a formidable looking foe. The word of God says, "When Saul and all Israel heard the words of the Philistine, they were dismayed, and greatly afraid" (1 Samuel 17:11). But God had a young boy whom he had prepared for such a time as this. His name was David, the son of Jesse.

David had three brothers who had joined King Saul's army. Their names were Eliab, the firstborn, and next to him Abinadab and the third was Shammah (1 Samuel 17:13). While the two armies were gathered, Jesse, David's father, sent the young David to his brothers with gifts of food. He was also told to find out how his older brothers were doing (1 Samuel 17:17-18). As David approached the battlefield he heard the railing voice of Goliath the champion of the Philistines. This so stirred the young David that he declared among the camp, "Who is this uncircumcised Philistine, that he should defy the armies of the living God?" (1 Samuel 17:26).

The response to David's visit was very cold by his older brother Eliab. In disdain he asked David, "Why are you here? Where did you leave those few sheep?" Eliab did not receive or respect his little brother David. In fact he was angry and despised him for even showing up to the battle. He didn't want David anywhere near him.

David was severally rejected by his brothers. Could it be that they remembered the visit from the Prophet Samuel who rejected them and anointed David? Eliab continued badgering David, "I know your pride and the naughtiness of your heart. Did you just come to the battle to watch?" (1 Samuel 17:28). David's brother falsely accused him of false motives, pride, and apathy, none of which was an accurate description of him. The rejected must learn what others think of them is not as important as what God thinks of them.

It must have been painful for David to be rejected by his oldest brother Eliab. After all, the younger sibling often looks up to and admires the older brother. David's reaction to Eliab's accusations was "What have I done now?" From this we learn that there must have been many times that his brothers were on him for one thing or another. David's response to Eliab is something the rejected can learn: "Is there not a cause? And he turned from him toward another" (1 Samuel 17:29-30). All of us will face false accusations from family members. David turned away from the rejection of his brother and stated his cause. Then he prophesied his future. Let's read this scripture.

"And he turned from him toward another, and spake after the same manner: and the people answered him again after the former manner. {31} And when the words were heard which David spake, they rehearsed them before Saul: and he sent for him. {32} And David said to Saul, Let no man's heart fail because of him; thy servant will go and fight with this Philistine. {33} And Saul said to David, Thou art not able to go against this Philistine to fight with him: for thou art but a youth, and he a man of war from his youth. {34} And David said unto Saul, Thy servant kept his father's sheep, and there came a lion, and a bear, and took a lamb out of the flock: {35} And I went out after him, and smote him, and delivered it out of his mouth: and when he arose against me, I caught him by his beard, and smote him, and slew him. {36} Thy servant slew both the lion and the bear: and this uncircumcised Philistine shall be as one of them, seeing he hath defied the armies of the living God. {37} David said moreover, The LORD that delivered me out of the paw of the lion, and out of the paw of the bear, he will deliver me out of the hand of this Philistine. And Saul said unto David, Go, and the LORD be with thee." (1 Samuel 17:30-37 KJV)

Rather than David taking his brother's accusations to heart, David focused on the larger picture. There wasn't time for a self-centered pity-party; God's people were being challenged. David simply turned away from his brother's false accusations. The rejected must discipline themselves to turn away from false accusations and pity-parties. David never considered his brother's comments. God had prepared David for "such a time as this." A new champion was about to be revealed to Israel. David did three things to overcome the power of rejection. These three things are important insights for us as we see that David...

> *turned away* from the false accusations of his brother and unto God's purpose.

> *stated his cause* and reason for living when he said, "Who is this uncircumcised Philistine that would challenge the armies of the living God?"

> *prophesied his future* by decreeing, "Thy servant slew both the lion and the bear: and this uncircumcised Philistine shall be as one of them, seeing he hath defied the armies of the living God."

These three actions are power tools of freedom to those who suffer from rejection. Are you ready to turn away, state your cause, and prophesy your future? In the next chapter we learn that rejection by a spouse can be one of the most painful events in life.

SUMMARY
SIBLING REJECTION

There are many times when sibling rivalry turns into abuse and sets children up to deal with issues of rejection in their life.

David was not received or respected by his brothers.

David's brother falsely accused him of false motives, pride, and apathy, none of which was an accurate description of him.

What others think about you is not as important as what God thinks about you.

David did not take his brothers accusations to heart but focused on the larger picture.

Turn away from false accusations and pity-parties.

David stated his cause, his reason for living.

David prophesied his future.

CHAPTER 7

SPOUSAL REJECTION

Rejection by a spouse can be one of the most painful events in life. Some have equated its pain to the death of a loved one. In this chapter, we will look at David being rejected by his wife Michal.

DAVID AND MICHAL

David had a deep experience with the Lord the day that he moved the ark of God's presence from Obed-edom's house into the city of Jerusalem. It was such an incredible event that David "danced before the Lord with all his might" (2 Samuel 6:14). How awesome it was to finally have God's presence in the city. Everyone must have been leaning out of his or her window shouting, "Glory to God in the highest!" All except one that is. When Michal, David's wife, saw her husband leaping and dancing in the streets, her response was very different.

> "And as the ark of the LORD came into the city of David, Michal Saul's daughter looked through a window, and saw king David leaping and dancing before the LORD; and she despised (*bazah*) him in her heart." (2 Samuel 6:16 KJV)

The word *despise* is *bazah* meaning to view as worthless. The spirit of rejection tries to make people feel as if they have no value. When the ark of the Lord was set in its place, David offered burnt offerings and peace offerings to the Lord. Then, he blessed the people in the name of the Lord of hosts. What an anointed service that must have been. In this faith-filled and joyous service, David blessed the people with bread and drink, and afterward left to bless his own home. Sadly, David is about to be rejected by his wife Michal. Let's read what she said.

> "Then David returned to bless his household. And Michal the daughter of Saul came out to

meet David, and said, How glorious was the king of Israel today, who uncovered himself to day in the eyes of the handmaids of his servants, as one of the vain fellows shamelessly uncovereth himself!" (2 Samuel 6:20 KJV).

Michal, the daughter of Saul, had rejected David's response (manner or expression of worship) to the Lord. Saul is a type of the religious spirit. Michal his daughter is a prophetic type of the fruit of a religious spirit. Religion never understands the heart-felt expression of the love of God. It is a thief of monumental proportions.

At that moment of rebuke by his wife, David faced the spirit of rejection. His wife had counted him as worthless. How David responds will determine his future. Will he submit to his religious wife's rebuke? Will he try to keep peace in his house by compromising his faith? Will he try to meet Michal halfway? Let's learn how we too can resist rejection through the example of David's response to Michal's rejection.

"And David said unto Michal, It was before the LORD, which chose me before thy father, and before all his house, to appoint me ruler over the people of the LORD, over Israel: therefore will I play before the LORD. {22}And I will yet be more vile than thus, and will be base in mine own sight: and of the maidservants which thou hast spoken of, of them shall I be had in honor. {23} Therefore Michal the daughter of Saul had no child unto the day of her death." (2 Samuel 6:21-23 KJV)

This scripture teaches us two important truths about resisting the spirit of rejection. First, David did not submit to the false accusations of his wife Michal. We are not who rejection says that we are. David did not compromise for peace. He held fast to the truth. To successfully resist rejection, we can never compromise our faith in God.

Secondly, David decreed his position in the kingdom. He declared, "It was the Lord who chose me ruler." We, too, must remember that we are seated in heavenly places in Christ Jesus. Because of our position in Christ, we are seated far away from the control of the spirit of rejection. We are above and not beneath! What He has done for us no man can take away.

> "And hath raised us up together, and made us sit together in heavenly places in Christ Jesus." (Ephesians 2:6 KJV)

David responded to Michal by saying, "Therefore I will play before the Lord and become more vile (Hebrew *qalal* meaning insignificant) than that." In other words, "If my expression of great joy looked trifling, insignificant, or below me, I will lower myself even further in God's presence." David teaches us a powerful truth with that statement. The lesson is that humility is a great weapon against the spirit of rejection. Humility is the opposite of pride or self-assertion. A humble person recognizes that his life is not his own.

> "What? know ye not that your body is the temple of the Holy Ghost which is in you, which ye have of God, and *ye are not your own?* {20} For ye are bought with a price: therefore glorify God in your body, and in your spirit, which are God's." (1 Corinthians 6:19-20 KJV Italics added)

Severe marriage problems and divorce are a leading cause of rejection. Many divorced people find it difficult to begin life again after divorce. They often struggle with feelings of failure and low self-esteem. It should also be pointed out that rejection is passed along throughout the family. Not only was David rejected by Michal, but he also rejected her. Apparently from this day forward, David and Michal refused to sleep with each other. As a result she bore him no children. I am sure that never being able to have children negatively affected Michal throughout her life.

SUMMARY
SPOUSAL REJECTION

God looks on the heart of man when he makes his decision to anoint someone.

To successfully resist rejection we can never compromise our faith in God.

Decree your position in the kingdom (Ephesians 2:6).

Our position in Christ has seated us far away from the control of the spirit of rejection.

CHAPTER 8

REJECTION BY CHILDREN

Absalom was the third son of David. He was born to Maacha, wife of David, and daughter of Tholmai, King of Gessur. Absalom was an incredibly good-looking young man with a full head of bushy black hair. David must have been quite proud of him. The first indication of an evil design is seen when Absalom murdered his older brother Amnon for raping his sister Tamar. Apparently, David heard of the rape but failed to punish the crime.

Sometimes when there is serious sin taking place in families, those with authority ignore what's going on or do nothing to stop the offenses. Somehow they think that not saying anything will protect the family from being shamed or dishonored. This creates an environment that Satan loves to work in.

RAPE AND REJECTION OF TAMAR

Let's read the testimony of the rape and rejection of Tamar. David's nonaction releases a tragic series of events throughout the family.

"And when she had brought them unto him to eat, he took hold of her, and said unto her, Come lie with me, my sister. {12} And she answered him, Nay, my brother, do not force me; for no such thing ought to be done in Israel: do not thou this folly. {13} And I, whither shall I cause my shame to go? and as for thee, thou shalt be as one of the fools in Israel. Now therefore, I pray thee, speak unto the king; for he will not withhold me from thee. {14} Howbeit he would not hearken unto her voice: but, being stronger than she, forced her, and lay with her. {15} Then Amnon hated her exceedingly;

so that the hatred wherewith he hated her was greater than the love wherewith he had loved her. And Amnon said unto her, Arise, be gone. {16} And she said unto him, There is no cause: this evil in sending me away is greater than the other that thou didst unto me. But he would not hearken unto her. {17} Then he called his servant that ministered unto him, and said, Put now this woman out from me, and bolt the door after her. {18} And she had a garment of divers colours upon her: for with such robes were the king's daughters that were virgins apparelled. Then his servant brought her out, and bolted the door after her. {19} And Tamar put ashes on her head, and rent her garment of divers colours that was on her, and laid her hand on her head, and went on crying." (2 Samuel 13:11-19 KJV)

From the above scriptures we learn of the rape of Tamar by her half brother Amnon. After the rape Amnon cannot stand his evil actions. He rejects Tamar by having his servants throw her out and bolt the door, thus locking her out of his presence. Tamar left the house totally devastated by the incident and fled to her brother Absalom.

Throughout my years of ministry, I have met people who were molested by a relative or a close friend of the family. Nonaction to protect a family member releases an air of mistrust throughout. Some of life's most painful rejection comes from childhood experiences. Rejection suffered in the early years often sets the tone for a person's entire life. Whenever a parent, grandparent, or someone we hold in esteem is not there for us, feelings of being unloved, unworthy, useless, defenseless, or insignificant can develop.

ABSALOM RESPONDS TO TAMAR

"And Absalom her brother said unto her, Hath Amnon thy brother been with thee? but hold now thy peace, my sister: he is thy brother; regard not this thing. So Tamar remained desolate (devastated) in her brother Absalom's house." (2 Samuel 13:20 KJV)

Absalom saw the distress that his sister Tamar was in. He questioned her and found out that Amnon had molested her. Absalom thought that surely dad would get involved, yet to no avail. But where was he?

Absalom must have viewed his father David's refusal to get involved in this family matter as a weakness and an excuse to take things into his own hands. After all, how could his father ignore a rape in the house? What about Tamar's feelings of abandonment? How do you think she felt about this? What about the nonaction of her father to help her? How could she have not felt the pains of rejection? Not only was she sexually violated by her own brother, but her father refused to get involved.

DAVID DOESN'T ACT

The scripture tells us that David was furious with the action of his son Amnon and the rape of his daughter Tamar, yet he did nothing to bring correction or justice. Why? Could it be that rejection was causing him to hide from further investigation?

> "But when king David heard of all these things, he was very wroth (furious)." (2 Samuel 13:21 KJV)

Abandonment or nonaction by a parent can lead to feelings of rejection. There is no biblical evidence that David ever consoled his daughter Tamar or dealt with Amnon on this issue.

Guilt of sexual abuse by others is a major avenue of rejection. Satan looks for anyway he can to keep rejection working throughout our families. David's past rejection experiences hindered him from getting involved with this painful family problem. But what we refuse to handle today will come back at us tomorrow.

David's own rejection caused a fear to hinder his involvement in his family's crisis. He did not handle his daughter's rape. Not only was David the king, he was also Dad. But where was Dad? Why wasn't he Tamar's advocate? Because of rejection David...

ignored a *very* serious issue.

passed rejection on to his daughter.

was afraid to confront a painful family situation.

did not exercise his authority as head of the house.

abandoned Tamar in her time of need.

lost the respect of his son Absalom.

David's judgement was severely impaired. Often the rejected will not confront those they love because they don't want to risk uncovering other pain that they buried deep within themselves. Rejection will cause you to hurt others who need your help.

BIRTHING OF BITTERNESS

For two years Absalom carried hatred in his heart toward his brother Amnon. David's nonaction released a root of bitterness in Absalom's heart against his father. Then one day Absalom displayed his cunning by inviting his father David and all of his brothers to a sheep shearing festival in a valley called Baalhazor in the land of Ephraim (2 Samuel 13:23). The first clip of the flocks were ordained for the priests (Deuteronomy 18:4), and the sacredness of the feast made it difficult for any member of the tribal family to absent himself.

"Now Absalom had commanded his servants, saying, Mark ye now when Amnon's heart is merry with wine, and when I say unto you, Smite Amnon; then kill him, fear not: have not

I commanded you? be coura-
geous, and be valiant. {29} And
the servants of Absalom did
unto Amnon as Absalom had
commanded. Then all the king's
sons arose, and every man got
him up upon his mule, and
fled." (2 Samuel 13:28-29 KJV)

David declined the invitation but
Absalom's brothers attended including
Amnon. Absalom instructed his servants to
watch Amnon and when he became drunk
to kill him. His servants did as he commanded them and murdered Amnon. It is
amazing to learn that bitterness (long held
resentment) can give birth to premeditated
murder. Absalom had his brother killed.

"And it came to pass, while they
were in the way, that tidings
came to David, saying, Absalom
hath slain all the king's sons,
and there is not one of them
left. {31} Then the king arose,
and tare his garments, and lay
on the earth; and all his servants stood by with their
clothes rent. {32} And Jonadab,
the son of Shimeah David's
brother, answered and said,
Let not my lord suppose that

they have slain all the young men the king's sons; for Amnon only is dead: for by the appointment of Absalom this hath been determined from the day that he forced his sister Tamar. {33} Now therefore let not my lord the king take the thing to his heart, to think that all the king's sons are dead: for Amnon only is dead." (2 Samuel 13:30-33 KJV)

David was incredibly wounded by this family tragedy. Family turmoil is a common cause for rejection to flourish. He had lost Amnon who was murdered by Absalom's servants. David may have been asking himself how one of his sons could take the life of his brother? How grieved he must have been. Those close to David said that they found him in mourning everyday. Even as I pen these words, I can feel a measure of his pain for his daughter and both of his sons. I wonder what the other family members were thinking.

"But Absalom fled. And the young man that kept the watch lifted up his eyes, and looked, and, behold, there came much people by the way of the hill

side behind him. {35} And
Jonadab said unto the king,
Behold, the king's sons come:
as thy servant said, so it is. {36}
And it came to pass, as soon as
he had made an end of speaking, that, behold, the king's
sons came, and lifted up their
voice and wept: and the king
also and all his servants wept
very sore." (2 Samuel 13:34-36
KJV)

ABSALOM FLEES
TO GRANDFATHER'S HOUSE

Absalom escaped the anger of his father
by seeking refuge in the home of his
maternal grandfather at Gessur. There he
hoped to remain until the grief of his father
died out. Then, he might be forgiven and
recalled to the royal court. But David did
not relent so quickly. After three years of
banishment, Absalom, through the
intervention of Joab, David's nephew and
trusted general, was allowed to return to
the city without being permitted to enter
the king's presence.

David's pain did not allow him to speak
with Absalom. Now David was rejecting
Absalom. Those with rejection oftentimes
refuse to deal with uncomfortable situations

by drawing into themselves and ignoring what's going on around them. We can never ignore the pain. Stored up pain will build a rejection personality that refuses to let you do the right thing. Remember the house that rejection builds? If David would have spoken to Absalom as a loving father, repented of his own sin of neglect and shortcomings, yet holding Absalom responsible, he may have stopped the tragic events that soon followed.

ABSALOM
RETURNS TO JERUSALEM

At some point in time, after Absalom returned to Jerusalem, he was restored to his former princely dignity and the apparent confidence of his father. Absalom began to undermine his father's credibility with the people. Absalom had lost respect for his father, and bitterness had entered his heart. He began slowly to steal the hearts of the people of Israel away from David and unto himself. Absalom refused to honor his father, but instead created an undercurrent of neglect, and fostered a discontent among the people. Satan looks for every opportunity of hurt, pain, bitterness, or unforgiveness to orchestrate our demise. For forty years Absalom held a grudge against his father, David, for not handling his sister's rape. Motivated by bitterness, he stole the hearts of the people.

ABSALOM BETRAYS DAVID

Then after forty years, Absalom lied to his father when he told him that he was going to go to Hebron to fulfill a self-imposed vow. After leaving, he incited a conspiracy against David (2 Samuel 15:12). He then began to unite hundreds of men with himself to overthrow his father's rule.

"See, I will tarry in the plain of the wilderness, until there come word from you to certify me. {29} Zadok therefore and Abiathar carried the ark of God again to Jerusalem: and they tarried there. {30} And David went up by the ascent of mount Olivet, and wept as he went up, and had his head covered, and he went barefoot: and all the people that was with him covered every man his head, and they went up, weeping as they went up. {31} And one told David, saying, Ahithophel is among the conspirators with Absalom. And David said, O

LORD, I pray thee, turn the counsel of Ahithophel into foolishness. {32} And it came to pass, that when David was come to the top of the mount, where he worshipped God, behold, Hushai the Archite came to meet him with his coat rent, and earth upon his head: {33} Unto whom David said, If thou passest on with me, then thou shalt be a burden unto me." (2 Samuel 15:28-33 KJV)

DAVID ESCAPES THE CAUDATE

When David got word of Absalom's caudate he fled for his life out of the city. The word declares that he left Jerusalem in tears (2 Samuel 15:30). What a tragic day this must have been. Can you imagine one of your children going to such great lengths to destroy you and your ministry? David must have asked himself many times, "Where did I go wrong with this boy?"

Absalom was full of bitterness, treachery, deceit, pride, arrogance, sedition, and murder, and he betrayed his father David. How did David get through this day? To leave all that he had worked so hard to gain, must have sorely worn against his heart.

In the face of all of this, the word says

71

that David submitted his life to God and began to worship him (2 Samuel 15:32). I can only imagine David's prayer as the sun was setting on the dark events of that day. Perhaps his prayer went something like this, "The LORD is my shepherd; I shall not want. {2} He maketh me to lie down in green pastures: he leadeth me beside the still waters. {3} He restoreth my soul: he leadeth me in the paths of righteousness for his name's sake. {4} Yea, though I walk through the valley of the shadow of death, I will fear no evil: for thou art with me; thy rod and thy staff they comfort me. {5} Thou preparest a table before me in the presence of mine enemies: thou anointest my head with oil; my cup runneth over. {6} Surely goodness and mercy shall follow me all the days of my life: and I will dwell in the house of the LORD forever" (Psalm 23 KJV). The only way to combat rejection is to gain a strong understanding of your position in Jesus Christ.

Not only was David rejected and betrayed by his son, but also hundreds of people who followed Absalom in his treachery. David had fought many wars so that Israel could live in peace. But now those who once praised him for his mighty deeds and gallantry turned their backs on him and joined a traitor.

As the story continues, we find Absalom's

treachery against his father did not succeed. Joab killed him when he was caught by his hair in the fork of a low hanging tree branch.

> "Then said Joab, I may not tarry thus with thee. And he took three darts in his hand, and thrust them through the heart of Absalom, while he was yet alive in the midst of the oak." (2 Samuel 18:14 KJV)

When David heard of Absalom's death he was deeply grieved. "And the king was much moved, and went up to the chamber over the gate, and wept: and as he went, thus he said, O my son Absalom, my son, my son Absalom! would God I had died for thee, O Absalom, my son, my son!" (2 Samuel 18:33).

DAVID'S UNCONTROLLABLE GRIEF

David did not handle his grief for Absalom properly in the midst of his people. Pain was coming out of David's heart through every tear. Rejection had hit its mark and taken him captive. I think that his cup was running over with grief.

Scripture teaches us that, "Word soon reached Joab that the king was weeping and mourning for Absalom. {2} As the troops heard of the king's deep grief for his son, the joy of that day's victory was turned into deep sadness. {3} They crept back into the city as though they were ashamed and had been beaten in battle. (4) The king covered his face with his hands and kept on weeping, "O my son Absalom! O Absalom, my son, my son!" (2 Samuel 19:1-4 NLT).

CORRECTION IS PROOF OF SONSHIP

David's grief was uncontrollable. He was suffering severely from the deep pain in his heart for the loss of another son. At that very moment, David could testify that 'Rejection was hell.' However, God had Joab, an old trusted general who had fought many battles with David, to correct him. Correction had to be given at a crucial time. David had to stop acting the way he was. Rejection was robbing the joy of victory from him and his men. "Then Joab went to the king's room and said to him, "We saved your life today and the lives of your sons, your daughters, and your wives and concubines. Yet you act like this, making us feel ashamed, as though we had done something wrong. {6} You seem to love those who hate you and hate those who love you (*misplaced loyalty*). You have made it clear today that we mean nothing to you. If Absalom had lived and all of us had died, you would be pleased. {7} Now go out there and congratulate the troops, for I swear by the LORD that if you don't, not a single one of them will remain here tonight. Then you will be worse off than you have ever been. {8} So the king went out and sat at the city gate, and as the news spread throughout the city that he was there, everyone went to him" (2 Samuel 19:5-8 NLT).

DAVID'S MISPLACED LOYALITY

David's uncontrollable grief and feelings of rejection caused a misplaced loyalty. At that very moment he was bound in self-centered anguish. Rejection had stolen his ability to see what was happening.

David found no sympathy from his old trusted friend, General Joab. He would not pet his flesh; rather Joab rebuked David for his pity-party and misplaced loyalty. David was weeping over Absalom and should have been rejoicing in their victory. It was vital that David express his appreciation to his men who had risked their lives to restore David back to the throne. He could not afford to let his rejection rob from his men. Because of the house that rejection built, David was not acting right. His personality was malfunctioning. Joab would have failed to help David had he offered David what he wanted, soulish sympathy, rather than what he needed, good solid counsel.

I have seen people do the very same thing right after a great victory. Instead of rejoicing in the success the Lord provided, they spoil the celebration with a display of woe-is-me. We can never let rejection stop us from doing the right thing. Rejection wants us to place our attention on the wrong things. Rejection misplaces our loyalty. If David had only received sympathy and soulish compassion he would have lost his kingdom.

SUMMARY
BETRAYAL BY CHILDREN

Some of life's most painful rejection comes from childhood experiences.

Rejection suffered in the early years often sets the tone for a person's entire life.

Whenever a parent, grandparent, or someone we hold in esteem rejects us, feelings of being unloved, unworthy, useless, or insignificant can develop.

Abandonment by a parent can lead to feelings of rejection.

Guilt of sexual abuse by others is a major avenue of rejection.

Family turmoil is a common cause for rejection to flourish.

Those with rejection oftentimes refuse to deal with uncomfortable situations by drawing into themselves and ignoring what's going on around them.

Stored up pain will build a rejection personality that refuses to let you do the right thing.

If David would have spoken to Absalom as a loving father, repented of his own inabilities and sin of neglect yet holding Absalom responsible, he may have stopped the tragic events that followed.

David found no sympathy from Joab. He would not pet his

flesh. Rather Joab rebuked David for his pity-party and misplaced loyalty.

Rejection wants us to place our attention on the wrong things.

If David had looked for sympathy and soulish compassion he would have lost his kingdom.

CHAPTER 9

REJECTION
BY CLOSE FRIENDS

Betrayal and abandonment seems to be running rampant in today's society. When someone very close to you rejects you, it is extremely painful. Many who I thought were close have left me without even so much as a good-bye. Once I met five daughters-in-law of a pastor all of whom were abandoned by their various fathers at a young age. Betrayal and abandonment are common weapons used to inflict the pain of rejection. Those who have been abandoned often feel empty, hopeless, and insecure. They view life, relationships, themselves and their future with uncertainty.

DAVID AND AHITHOPHEL

David experienced the pain of betrayal and abandonment when his counsel and close friend Ahithophel, grandfather of Bathsheba, joined the revolt of his traitorous son Absalom (2 Samuel 15:12). David said, "Yea, mine own familiar friend, in whom I trusted, which did eat of my bread, hath lifted up his heel against me" (Psalms 41:9 KJV). Not only did David have to press through the pain of his son Absalom betraying him but now his most trusted companion turned his back on him too. David must have been crushed by this series of events, yet God gave David strength to continue on. After searching the scriptures I think the following best captures the anguish of betrayal and abandonment that David felt.

> "My heart is sore pained within me: and the terrors of death are fallen upon me. {5} Fearfulness and trembling are come upon me, and horror hath overwhelmed me. {6} And I said, Oh that I had wings like a dove! for then would I fly away, and be at rest. {7} Lo, then would I wan-

der far off, and remain in the wilderness. Selah." (Psalms 55:4-7 KJV)

David was hurt by the betrayal of his closest friend Ahithophel. The scripture above explains how David must have felt. David was "sore pained." This means that there was a gut-wrenching grief inside of him. He just wanted to "fly away." Those with rejection just want to escape pain by running or hiding. Just like David, they would rather "remain in the wilderness" than face life anymore.

"For it was not an enemy that reproached me; then I could have borne it: neither was it he that hated me that did magnify himself against me; then I would have hid myself from him: {13} But it was thou, a man mine equal, my guide, and mine acquaintance. {14} We took sweet counsel together, and walked unto the house of God in company." (Psalms 55:12-14 KJV)

Not only was Ahithophel David's close companion, but they also went to church together. Just as those who have been hurt by church leaders, many have been hurt by those they worshipped alongside.

> "He hath put forth his hands against such as be at peace with him: he hath broken his covenant. {21} The words of his mouth were smoother than butter, but war was in his heart: his words were softer than oil, yet were they drawn swords." (Psalms 55:20-21 KJV)

David said that his friend violated his trust and their friendship. He had broken their covenant because there was "war in his heart."

> "Cast thy burden upon the LORD, and he shall sustain thee: he shall never suffer the righteous to be moved. {23} But thou, O God, shalt bring them down into the pit of destruction: bloody and deceitful men shall not live out half their days; but I will trust in thee." (Psalms 55:22-23 KJV)

THREE KEYS TO FREEDOM

Moreover, David gives us some great insight in deflecting the pain of betrayal and abandonment. Let's look at the three things that David did.

First, David "cast his burden on the Lord." The word *cast* is Hebrew *shalak* meaning to...

throw

hurl

fling

shed

cast off.

Scripture tells us that Jesus "took our infirmities and bore our sicknesses" (Matthew 8:17 KJV). One of the most helpful prayers to pray when hurt is, "Lord I cast all my cares on you because I know that you care for me" (1 Peter 5:7).

Secondly, David confesses the word of God over his life. He declares, "He shall sustain me and never suffer the righteous to be moved (shaken)." The word *sustain* (Hebrew *kuwl*) means to...

hold-up

nourish

refresh

support

supply.

Next, David confesses that he doesn't understand why all of these things are happening to him but he boldly says, "Yet will I trust God." As painful as betrayal and abandonment are, we can still depend on Jesus to help us get through it all. The rejected must do what David did when he cried out to the Lord in prayer and declared God to be his refuge and his reason for living.

"Maschil of David; A Prayer when he was in the cave. I cried unto the LORD with my voice; with my voice unto the LORD did I make my supplication. {2} I poured out my complaint before him; I showed before him my trouble. {3} When my spirit was overwhelmed within me, then thou knewest my path. In the way wherein I walked have they privily laid a snare for me. {4} I looked on my right hand, and beheld, but there was no man that would know me: refuge failed me; no man cared for my soul. {5} I cried unto thee, O LORD: I said, Thou art my refuge and my portion in the land of the living. {6} Attend unto my cry; for I am brought very low: deliver me from my persecutors; for they are stronger than I. {7} Bring my soul out of prison, that I may praise thy name: the righteous shall compass me about; for thou shalt deal bountifully with me." (Psalms 142 KJV)

SUMMARY
BETRAYED AND ABANDONED BY CLOSE FRIENDS

Betrayal and abandonment are common weapons used to inflict the pain of rejection.

The word *cast* is Hebrew *shalak* meaning to throw, hurl, fling, shed, cast off.

One of the most helpful prayers to pray when hurt is, "Lord I cast all my cares on you because I know that you care for me" (1 Peter 5:7).

The word *sustain* (Hebrew *kuwl*) means to hold-up, nourish, refresh, support and supply.

CHAPTER 10

ME, CHOSEN AND ACCEPTED?

F reedom from rejection is essential for spiritual growth. Those who suffer with it always feel that their self-worth is lacking. God has uniquely created us in such a way that we have the ability to lay-hold of an identity and attach value to it. Many times that identity does not come from Christ but from rejection. After an identity is created we can step back, examine it, and decide if we like it or not. After reading this book, there may be an identity created by rejection that you may want to exchange. Applying the knowledge of the word of God in your life can change the way you perceive yourself. Your feelings and perceptions of value can be renovated with truth. The critical voice of rejection (internalization) that constantly tears down your value can be disarmed. Benefiting from this book is not as simple as just reading it. You will have to do some work. Don't get disappointed! You have already begun. There are new understandings, exercises, and skills that you will need to lay-hold of. Make a commitment right now to chart a course for freedom. The feelings of rejection need to be replaced by the understanding that we are totally accepted by the Lord.

ACCEPTED AND NOT REJECTED

You are accepted just as you are and not rejected. These are always comforting words to those fighting the tormenting feelings of rejection.

> "Of a truth I perceive that God is no respecter of persons: {35} But in every nation he that feareth him, and worketh righteousness, is *accepted with him.* (Acts 10:34-35 KJV Italics added)

It is important for those who suffer with rejection to know that God has not rejected them. They must learn to *exchange* the feelings of rejection with the knowledge of acceptance. God never intended for us to struggle with feelings of low self-esteem, unworthiness, or rejection. Jesus wants us to understand that we have value and worth, not because of who we are in ourselves, but because of who we are in Jesus. When we fail to accept ourselves in Him, rejection has an open door to our emotions.

Dealing successfully with rejection requires honesty and a willingness to pull out all of the roots of our pain including a poor view of our self-worth. We can never base our worth as a person on the opinion of others. Nor can we confuse position, titles, works, or status with worth. We are valuable! Jesus thought enough of us to die on the cross for us. We are not our own. We belong to Him (1 Corinthians 6:19-20).

Oftentimes at the church, I see people struggle with rejection when they do not qualify for a particular position of helps in the ministry. In no way does that devaluate them, yet they seem to confuse position with personal value. Throughout the years I have seen people leave the ministry because they did not get a 'coveted position' in the church. This is a grievous thing. Our self-worth or person-hood should never be determined by our social position in life. Anytime we base our self-worth on what other people say about us, or our social position in life, we set ourselves up for rejection.

GOD'S OWN POSSESSION

In his first epistle, Peter wrote to a group of believers who were struggling with persecution and deep rejection. Trying to instill a sense of hope in those who would read his letter, Peter told them of their value in the kingdom of God:

> "You are a chosen race, a royal priesthood, a holy nation, a people for God's own possession, that you may proclaim the excellencies of Him who has called you out of darkness into His marvelous light; for you once were not a people, but now you are the people of God; you had not received mercy, but now you have received mercy." (1 Peter 2:9-10 KJV)

Chosen, royal, holy, and God's very own possession – wow! Peter also lets everyone know that they were special in the eyes of the Lord. They were accepted and not rejected. Let's learn to exchange our feelings of rejection for a solid knowing that we are accepted by the Lord Himself. Scripture assures us that we are the "accepted in the beloved" (Ephesians 1:6).

When you begin to feel rejected, verbally pray this prayer: "Thank you, Jesus, that I am accepted and not rejected. You have declared me to be chosen, royal, holy, and your very own. I am worthy, valuable, useful, and totally accepted. Right now I exchange these feelings of rejection for the knowledge of the truth; you loved me enough to die for me and I love you enough to live for you."

SUMMARY
ME, CHOSEN AND ACCEPTED?

Freedom from rejection is essential for spiritual growth.

One must learn to *exchange* the feelings of rejection with the knowledge of acceptance.

When we fail to accept ourselves in Jesus, rejection has an open door to our emotions.

We can never base our worth as a person on the opinion of others. Nor can we confuse position, titles, works, or status with worth.

Our self-worth or person-hood is never determined by our

social position in life. Anytime
we base our self-worth on what
other people say about us, or
our social position in life, we
set ourselves up for rejection.

CHAPTER 11

OH NO! NOT CORRECTION

If there is any thing that the rejected can not stand it would be correction. Most suffering with rejection would rather take a beating with a stick than be corrected. The rejected take correction as an attack against their value. For some twisted reason, correction undermines their sense of self-worth. However, correction is very valuable to everybody. The rejected must recognize the value of correction and covet it. Without correction we can never learn new skills, or develop emotionally and grow.

Resistance to correction severely hinders one's ability to mature. God has a cure for this hindrance to our development. Scripture declares, "God hath set some in the church, first apostles, secondarily prophets, thirdly teachers" to help us to grow (1 Corinthians 12:18). These ministries are also referred to as ascension gifts. When Jesus ascended into heaven he sent back gifts to men. These gifts were given to the body of Christ by Jesus himself. Their ministry calling is to bring every believer into a place of spiritual maturity and activation (Ephesians 4). To be *mature* means to be fully...

developed

aged

completed.

Because of the ministry of the ascension gifts to bring about a full development of believers there will always be a demand put upon us to grow. Personal growth and maturity is vital for us if we are to complete the Great Commission. However, for us to mature from babes in Christ to sons of God, correction is necessary. There is no escaping the issue.

TRANSITION

True ministers of the gospel have a father's heart. The father has the best interest of the son in his heart. The assignment of a father is to *transition* his son into adulthood by preparing him to successfully deal with the responsibilities of life.

In this world we have natural fathers and spiritual fathers. The Apostle Paul said, "For though ye have ten thousand instructors in Christ, yet have ye not many fathers" (1 Corinthians 4:15). The success and well-being of Paul's spiritual sons like Timothy was always in his heart. For Paul to be able to help Timothy or others, they had to be willing to submit to any counsel and correction that Paul would offer. If Paul's spiritual sons were suffering with rejection they would not have been able to fulfill their ministries.

CORRECTION BRINGS ADVANCEMENT

There are several reasons why children resist correction, including rebellion, rejection, and self-centeredness. Once a young lady told me that 'she should not have to do anything that she did not want to do.' Her statement captured the essence of my inability to help her mature. Today she still lives in rebellion away from God. My heart goes out to her because of the mighty call of God upon her life that sits awaiting her obedience.

95

Another one of my spiritual sons told me that he wanted to 'grow at his own pace.' Twelve years later he is still in the same pitiful condition. Without godly counsel and loving correction, from those whom God has placed over us we cannot arise to the next level.

TRAINING INSTRUCTION AND CORRECTION

Through correction, all of us can advance to a level beyond our current abilities. Without learning from our mistakes and failures, there can be no advancement. We simply could not grow. The word of God speaks much about correction.

> "And ye have forgotten the exhortation which speaketh unto you as unto children, My son, despise not thou the chastening of the Lord, nor faint when thou art rebuked of him: {6} For whom the Lord loveth he chasteneth, and scourgeth every son whom he receiveth. {7} If ye endure chastening, God dealeth with you as with sons; for what son is he whom the father chasteneth not? {8} But if ye be without chastisement,

whereof all are partakers, then are ye bastards, and not sons. {9} Furthermore we have had fathers of our flesh which corrected us, and we gave them reverence: shall we not much rather be in subjection unto the Father of spirits, and live? {10} For they verily for a few days chastened us after their own pleasure; but he for our profit, that we might be partakers of his holiness. {11} Now no chastening for the present seemeth to be joyous, but grievous: nevertheless afterward it yieldeth the peaceable fruit of righteousness unto them which are exercised thereby." (Hebrews 12: 5-11 KJV)

The word *chastening* is the Greek word *paidiuo* meaning to...

train

instruct

cause to learn

mold

correct.

Those with rejection take every thing way too personal. That is why they have a difficult time with correction. Correction seems to make them feel less than a person. Rejection tells the person that correction is a direct assault against their sense of value. They perceive correction as a threat to tear down their self-esteem. However, in reality, all must learn the value of correction. Correction always prepares us for advancement.

CORRECTION IS PROOF OF SONSHIP

When we are chastened (corrected) by God, either through His word, His leaders, or through difficult circumstances, it is not a sign of His rejecting us, but His receiving us. God's goal is not to make us miserable, but rather to correct us for our own good. *Chastening is proof of sonship.* The word declares, "My son, despise not the chastening of the LORD; neither be weary of his correction: {12} For whom the LORD loveth he correcteth; even as a father the son in whom he delighteth" (Proverbs 3:11-12 KJV). If God did not love you, then He would not take the time to correct you.

"As many as I love, I rebuke
(convict) and chasten (correct);
be zealous (earnestly pursue)
therefore, and repent (change
your mind)." (Revelation 3:19
KJV)

Unfortunately there is a counterfeit idea
of love that Satan has sold the church. Some
wrongly think, because God is love, that they
should never be corrected. Satan has told
people that they should be received and
maintained, as is, in a spirit of love that is
not real. When you truly love someone, you
will not leave him or her in the condition
they are in. To allow a person to be ruled
by their feelings, and never be challenged
to move into faith and character
development, would not be love. If one is
not teachable, he will be hindered. If he is
not teachable, he will be hindered from
growing and maturing in the Lord. Beloved,
it is time for all of us to grow up into the
fullness of our calling. We are not to remain
children of God, but become sons of God.
The next time God uses your pastor to
correct you remember, "Correction is proof
of sonship and the prerequisite for
advancement." It is not an attack against
your value.

SUMMARY
OH NO! NOT CORRECTION

The rejected take correction as an attack against their value.

The rejected must recognize the value of correction and covet it.

Through correction all of us can advance to a level beyond our current abilities.

Without learning from our mistakes and failures there can be no advancement.

The word *chastening* is the Greek word *paidiuo* meaning to train, instruct, mold, correct, and cause to learn.

When we are chastened (corrected) by God, either through His word, His leaders, or through difficult circumstances, it is not a sign of His rejecting us, but His receiving us.

Correction is not an attack against your value.

CHAPTER 12

MINISTERING TO THOSE WITH REJECTION

Identification is a very important part of ministering to those with rejection. *Identification* means to put oneself in another's place by understanding and sharing the thoughts, feelings, emotions, and problems of another. Intercession is a form of identification. Identification is closely related to and often mistaken for carnal sympathy. There is a great difference in 'feeling sorry' for someone and identifying with them in an effort to help them.

REACH OUT AND TOUCH ME

Jesus identifies with our suffering. He is our great example of bringing healing to those in need. "For we have not a high priest which cannot be *touched with the feeling* of our infirmities; but was in all points tempted like as we are, yet without sin" (Hebrews 4:15 KJV Italics added). We too can be touched with the feelings of others. The Greek expression for "touched with the feeling" is *sumpatheo* meaning to...

have compassion.

be affected with the same feeling as another.

sympathize with.

feel for.

identify with.

From the Greek word *sumpatheo* we get our English word sympathy. Jesus' sympathy is not feeling sorry for us only, but a way of compassionately identifying with our suffering to bring about healing and deliverance.

It is important to those who suffer the pain of rejection, that we identify with their pain. This may sound trivial, but for you to be an effective minister it is essential. Identification is the bridge that will connect you to the rejected.

Identifying with the pain of the rejected will prequalify you as a minister in their eyes. Pain speaks to the rejected asking them if you can 'feel their pain.' If not, then they will disqualify you to minister to them.

NEGATIVE IDENTIFICATION

The negative side to identification on the part of the rejected is the error of seeking out soulish sympathy, consolation and solace, from those with common ground. You can console someone without ever helping one get free.

Oftentimes those with rejection search for others with the same hurts and wounds (common ground) to sympathize with them. Unfortunately, controllers also look for those suffering with rejection. Jezebel easily identifies with one's pain, hurts and wounds. She will use them to control the person, not to set them free. A true minister of the gospel will never feed into hurts and wounds. The blind can never lead the blind, least they both fall into a ditch (Luke 6:39).

VALUE OF IDENTIFICATON

Let me explain the value of identification with a couple of examples. We replaced some light fixtures in our church building including two in my office. Of all the lights that we replaced in the entire building, the ones in my office would not work correctly. Of course, this really aggravated me because I had lots of work to do and was hindered because I couldn't see very well. My wife came into the room, and I began to vent my frustration with the lights to her. Her response was that she didn't want to hear about it. In fact, she was quite short with me. I was taken back by her lack of concern for my perilous dilemma. Didn't she think that I had some important work to do? After all, wasn't I the senior pastor? Then I found myself getting angry with her. I began transferring my frustration with the lights toward her. As I thought about my anger toward her for not 'understanding my feelings,' I experienced rejection's operations. Negative feelings plague those who suffer with rejection. If they don't think that you are identifying with their pain, then you cannot minister to them. To those with rejection, the bridge of communication (identification) is destroyed when you don't feel the pain.

I learned an interesting lesson from this event. When my wife did not *identify* with my aggravation, I felt that she was not connected to me. My negative emotions were offering a bridge to her that she refused to walk on. *Rejection tells you that your feelings are the real you.* In other words, my feelings (rejection) were telling me because she was not identifying with my aggravation (pain) that I was not important. She just blew me off with a trivial, "I'm too busy to deal with the lights right now." To her it meant that we could handle it later. To me it was an attack against my value.

When you are counseling with a person with rejection personality malfunctions, make sure that you take the time to connect with their pain. Let them spend some time and try their best to explain their feelings. It's important to them that you make an attempt to understand them. Not to have a co-pity-party with them but to start the healing process off right. Rejection is a sneaky thing. The rejected need to know that you are making the attempt to identify with them.

I can't write an exhaustive work on how a person gets hurt. Suffice it to say that the very heart of the rejection personality malfunction is some sort of pain. Yes, everybody faces rejection constantly, but the person who has been hurt and wounded will respond to rejection circumstances differently than those being rejected who have not been hurt. If we can remove the pain and exchange feelings for truth, then we can heal the person. Some people are healed instantly from pain while others take more time. Remember, Jesus is our great physician and we can depend on his help.

POINT TOWARD JESUS

Once a dear friend got a divorce. It was a heart-wrenching experience for him. He tried desperately to save his marriage to no avail. One day he told me that he went to his church where they were promoting a single's ministry. Since he was now single he was interested in getting on with his life and dealing with the issues that now faced him as a single believer. However, to his surprise, the leader of the group announced during the first meeting that divorced persons could not attend the class. This event of not being included (rejected) brought to the surface (flashbacks) his pain. He told me that he felt like he was somehow diminished in value because of his divorce. Even though I have been happily married for twenty-five years and have never been divorced, I identified with his pain and pointed him to Jesus. Then I prayed for him and reassured him that God was still the "author and finisher of his faith" (Hebrews 12:2). After I prayed for him, I put my arms around him and told him that I loved him too.

When ministering to those being freed

from hurts, always point them to Jesus who understands them better than anyone else. Today my friend is happily married to a woman who really loves him and they are both serving God. Those suffering from rejection must lay-hold of the unchanging truth that we are unconditionally loved, totally accepted, and complete in Christ.

PRAYING FOR THE REJECTED

When I pray for people with inner hurts and wounds there is such a love and compassion that overcomes me. Through the anointing, it seems like I can reach into the very depths of their heart and grab hold of that pain and pull it out. True compassion for the hurting is always coupled with an urge from the Holy Spirit to help them get free.

It is important to offer more than pity to those who are afflicted with rejection and pray for them. Remember that the root cause of rejection is some sort of pain. Deliverance is an important key in the process of helping someone who is struggling from the fruit of rejection. Some things that should be bound in deliverance prayer are as follows:

self-rejection

abandonment

abuse of all kinds

hurts and wounds

false personality

discouragement

anxiety

suspicion

non trust

fear of people's opinion

fear of failure

insecurity

bitterness

shame

guilt

condemnation

unworthiness.

Binding up the items above is a good start when you pray for someone suffering from rejection. For an in-depth study of the scriptural foundations for deliverance read my book *Come Out!* 1 I wrote this book as a handbook for the serious deliverance minister. It is a valuable asset to your ministerial library. It has helped hundreds of precious people get free.

SUMMARY
MINISTERING TO THOSE WITH
REJECTION

Identification means to put oneself in another's place; to understand and share the thoughts, feelings, emotions, and problems of another.

The Greek expression for "touched with the feeling" is *sumpatheo* meaning to have compassion, be affected with the same feeling as another, sympathize with and feel for (Hebrews 4:15).

Jesus' sympathy is not feeling sorry for us only but a way of compassionately identifying with our suffering to bring about healing and deliverance.

Oftentimes those with rejection search for others with the same hurts and wounds (common ground) to sympathize with them.

Rejection tells you that your feelings are the real you.

When ministering to those being freed from hurts, always point them to Jesus who understands them better than anyone else (Hebrews 12:2).

Those suffering from rejection must lay-hold of the unchanging truth that we are unconditionally loved, totally accepted, and complete in Christ.

Deliverance is an important key in the process of helping someone who is struggling from the fruit of rejection.

Notes

1 Jonas Clark, "Come Out," (Hallandale, FL. Spirit of Life Publications, 2001)

CHAPTER 13

THE GATES
OF UNFORGIVENESS

Many people have been so hurt that they are locked in the pit of rejection and don't know how to escape. I am convinced that the hell of rejection has reinforced gates caused by unforgiveness and bitterness. So, how can one escape? The answer is found in our ability to forgive.

Consider Brian who has a powerful testimony regarding forgiveness and rejection. Brian lived in a large family with eight brothers and sisters. When Brian was five years old his mother and father separated and he was left with his older sisters to raise him.

Since Brian was only five years old, he could not understand why his mother left

111

him. He felt unwanted and unimportant. Now as a single mother, she faced the challenges of raising all the children by herself. She moved to another city looking for work and needed time to prepare a place for the children to follow her. It was four long years before Brian saw his mother again. After being reunited with his mother he and his siblings lived together.

When Brian was seventeen years old his father moved back into the house in an attempt to reconcile with his mother. The effort proved fruitless and failed miserably. There were many nights of severe arguments and chaos throughout the household, and the family split. Some of the children sided with the father and others sided with the mother. Brian told me that he felt divided and torn in the middle. About that time Brian gave his life to Jesus and was powerfully changed. When he tried to share the gospel with his family, they rejected it and would not receive from him.

Throughout Brian's teenage years he was overweight and one of his brothers teased him incessantly. Brian was so hurt by this chiding that he would cry himself to sleep at night. He felt so alone in that house, even though it was full of people. Brian even thought that his family was not really his family. He wanted to run away from home and look for his real family. After all, how could this be his real family? Brian told me that he often dreamed about what his real mother and family would be like if he found them. Even though Brian was born again he was still suffering from rejection. Without a conscious understanding, he was still harboring unforgiveness and bitterness in his heart toward his mother.

Brian began to attend church on a regular basis. He liked what he was hearing and felt drawn to be around other believers. One night at church a lady was speaking about the baptism in the Holy Spirit and the importance of forgiving those who had hurt them. At that moment his heart was compelled to forgive his brother for the constant teasing. When Brian forgave his brother he was instantly filled with the Holy Spirit and began to speak in other tongues.

In the days to follow the Holy Spirit continued to deal with Brian's heart about forgiving others. Soon he found himself in a serious argument with his mother. They were yelling and screaming at one another. Then Brian yelled, "Mom, you have never told me that you loved me!" His mother was shocked and stunned. The look on her face was a puzzled amazement. When she heard those words she began to breakdown and cry. Then she said, "Son, I do love you."

Brian went seventeen years without a single "I love you" from his mother. When

Brian heard those words and saw his mother's tears, he, too, broke down and cried. It was at that moment that he forgave his mother. Through Brian's tears flowed years of pain and hurt. That night the rejection was broken and Brian began to grow and mature in the Lord. Someone may have hurt you deeply, but by forgiving them, you free yourself to receive God's forgiveness and restoration in your own life.

THE FORGIVING CHOICE

When you were born again you received the ability to forgive. It became a part of your new nature (2 Corinthians 5:17). Before we describe what forgiveness is, perhaps we should first mention what forgiveness is not. Forgiveness is not denial, condoning, excusing, condemning, seeking justice, or reconciliation. We should not confuse reconciliation with forgiveness. Reconciliation is when *two* people who have separated because of a disagreement come back together. Therefore, it is possible for you to forgive someone without ever obtaining reconciliation. It takes two people to reconcile, but only one person to offer forgiveness. So then, forgiveness is a choice we make through the use of our wills.

Offering forgiveness has absolutely nothing to do with our feelings. To forgive we simply *choose* to obey God's word, "forgive those who have trespassed against us" (see Matthew 6:12). Forgiveness is not an emotion; it is a decision. God is very serious about the issue of forgiveness. He even teaches us that if we do not forgive, then our heavenly Father will not forgive.

> "For if ye forgive men their trespasses, your heavenly Father will also forgive you: {15} But if ye forgive not men their trespasses, neither will your Father forgive your trespasses" (Matthew 6:14-15 KJV).

We can never allow unforgiveness to lock us up in the past. God sent his only begotten son to die in our place so that our sins, faults, and failings could be freely forgiven. As children of God, he expects us to offer the same forgiveness to those who have sinned against us. Jesus said, "For in the same way you judge others, you will be judged, and with the measure you use, it will be measured to you" (Matthew 7:2). You can't store up good feelings toward those whom you have forgiven, you can only draw them fresh from God each day. The Holy Spirit is here to help us to forgive those who have hurt us. Forgiveness is an essential key that will free you from the pain of rejection.

115

SUMMARY
THE GATES OF
UNFORGIVENESS

When you were born again you received the ability to forgive. It became a part of your new nature (2 Corinthians 5:17).

Forgiveness is not denial, condoning, excusing, condemning, seeking justice, or reconciliation.

Reconciliation is when *two* people who have separated because of a disagreement come back together.

It is possible for you to forgive someone without ever obtaining reconciliation. It takes two people to reconcile but only one person to offer forgiveness.

Forgiveness is a choice that we make through the use of our wills.

Offering forgiveness has absolutely nothing to do with our feelings.

116

To forgive we simply *choose* to obey God's word, "forgive those who have trespassed against us" (see Matthew 6:12).

Forgiveness is an essential key that will free you from the pain of rejection.

CHAPTER 14

THE MR. HYDE SYNDROME

I have passed through many personality malfunctions in my life caused from the pain of rejection. This qualifies me, to some degree, to deal with a rejected belief system that stops us from breaking through. In this chapter, I am not going to pull any punches but will get right to the point. The rejected personality is a self-centered, rude, impertinent, non-civil, Mr. Hyde personality! I know that sounds a bit harsh, but the rejected know that it is true.

We can study all about the emotional scars of yesterday, come to the understanding that we have a problem with rejection, and feel sorry for ourselves, but never change. Or, we can make a decision to overcome the non-civil personality that rejection has built. The decision to change is not up to someone else; that decision is up to us. Will it be uncomfortable? Will freedom require us to change? The answer to both questions is, "Yes." But why continue to live the way you are living? Life is more than you can see right now.

To change means that we must break the repetitive patterns that have caused us to be the rude and self-centered people that we have become. How is it that a person who suffers from rejection can function at work but on a personal level is a real basket case? Is it because work is mechanical and relationships are more emotional? Or could it just be caused by a totally self-centered view of life?

People learn and grow emotionally as a process of interaction with others. However, the rejected will intentionally avoid emotional interactions. I have met many with rejection problems that had terrible people skills. They have a very difficult time communicating and often withdraw themselves into a cocoon.

For example, some isolate themselves in another room when family or others visit. Sometimes this is because they have a fear of communicating inadequately. At other times the isolation is simply the result of the self-centered, non-civil, rejection personality. If you don't want to talk about *their* interest, then they don't want to talk with you at all. To escape the forced interaction with others they say things like, "That's your company." The result is they hide in their cave and never grow emotionally.

Yes, I know that the rejected are touchy, overly sensitive, and avoid emotional exercises with others. But I also know that they wear their feelings on their shoulders and can be extremely rude. Because they have spent years guarding the rejection, they are simply lacking in plain, old-fashioned, good manners.

It doesn't matter how hurt you have been. To tear down the house that rejection built, you are going to have to learn some basic manners and people skills. You can start by being polite to others, even if you don't 'feel' like it. Remembering the golden rule will help you significantly, "Do unto others as you would have them do unto you."

Now is the time to tear down the Dr. Jekyll and Mr. Hyde personality and start developing some basic people skills. Being courteous, kind, thoughtful, agreeable and friendly may be foreign to you, but if you really want to change, they must become part of your new self. You have been uncivil long enough. Just look at being thoughtful as a social responsibility that you can never afford to overlook again.

From now on don't underestimate the value of good manners and basic social skills, which will smooth out the rough edges that rejection has built. No one is born with communication or people skills. Learn to be polite and consider the feelings of others. Come out of the cave of ill manners and force yourself to grow. Everything improves with practice, including civility. Tell the Mr. Hyde personality good-bye.

ENABLERS

For a person to remain emotionally immature there must be a series of enablers throughout their life. I once knew a successful businessman who was very self-centered and emotionally immature because of rejection. As we take a look at his life, we will notice a series of enablers who refused to help him grow up.

The first enablers we discover in the man's life were his parents. When he was a child his parents never took the time to discipline and correct his self-centered behavior. His father was seldom home and when he was, he was of little help in disciplining the child. Because of parental neglect he grew up full of emotional maladies. His people skills were never developed; he did not respect others, and often suffered from severe bouts of depression.

As a young man he married a woman and they had a child together. His wife refused to allow his self-centered behavior to go unchecked. Whenever she attempted to help stabilize him emotionally, he took it as an attack against his self-worth and would lash out at her. She felt that the burden to maintain his happiness was her responsibility. Conflict was common place in their home. The man became very self-centered, controlling, and domineering. Then the man began to abuse his wife both emotionally and physically. Nine years of turmoil led to a divorce. Most of the conflict in the home was because the man wanted to do whatever he liked without regard to the feelings of others.

The next enablers we will find are the man's employees. Many who suffer with rejection are very hard workers. They identify self-worth and value with accomplishments. After the man's divorce he immersed himself in his work and became very wealthy. His wealth created a prominence in his own eyes. Even though he was now wealthy, his wealth was a license to continue living in an uncivil and disrespectful manner. People that worked for him tolerated his insolence and abuse because they needed their paycheck. Unfortunately his employees also continued to be enablers. Those who refused to submit to his abuse would either quit or get fired. As the years passed the man got worse and worse.

The final enabler we find in his life was Jezebel. A few years later this man married a woman who was the classic Jezebel gold-digger. She married him for his money and allowed him to continue on in his emotional immaturity. She was good at handling the things that he didn't like to handle. She would even handle his dirty work for him; thus the classic Ahab and Jezebel relationship. The man died shortly after. Jezebel got his money and stole the man's only child's inheritance.

SUMMARY
THE MR. HYDE SYNDROME

The rejected personality is a self-centered, rude, impertinent, non-civil, and Mr. Hyde personality!

We can study all about the emotional scars of yesterday, come to the understanding that we have a problem with rejection, and feel sorry for ourselves, but never change.

To *change* means that we must break the repetitive patterns that have caused us to be the rude and self-centered people that we have become.

The rejected are touchy, overly sensitive, and avoid emotional exercises with others.

Oftentimes the rejected wear their feelings on their shoulders and can often be extremely rude.

To tear down the house that rejection built, you are going to have to learn some basic manners and people skills. You can start by being polite to others, even if you don't 'feel' like it.

The golden rule will help those with rejection malfunction personality significantly, "Do unto others as you would have them do unto you."

For a person to remain emotionally immature there must be a series of enablers throughout their life.

CHAPTER 15

UNDOING REJECTION

The rejected sometimes cast blame, get angry and offended, and then erect defense barriers around themselves. Others bury themselves in their work. Still others make excuses for living and turn to alcohol, drugs or food to subdue their pain and emotional distress. The unwillingness to face uncertain pain leads to addictions. Even though the use of drugs, alcohol and other substances provide a short-term relief from pain they eventually do severe damage by enabling destructive patterns, thus making the pain worse.

THE FAMOUS DISAPPEARING ACT

Then we find those who totally disappear

from the radar screen. Their attitude is, "If you want to see me then stop what you are doing and send out the search party." Those suffering from rejection are notorious for disappearing from sight.

In aviation it is required that one close out a filed flight plan upon arrival at their intended destination. If a pilot fails to do so, the authorities send out a search and rescue party. Air traffic controllers can't handle any disappearing acts from pilots. There are times when pilots forget to cancel their flight plan, later finding themselves in serious trouble with the FAA and facing potentially hefty fines.

The rejected are also known to disappear from your airspace. When they are internalizing feelings of rejection and flying with the woe-is-me auto-pilot engaged, you might not see them for weeks. "What's happening?" you ask. They are practicing their famous disappearing act. This is how they deal with their negative emotions and feelings of rejection. They enter a hide-and-seek routine where they expect you to send out the search party and chase them down. The chase seems to give them a sense of value and appreciation. If you don't find them, they don't think you love them or they become indifferent. The rejected will use this chase scene to test your love for them. If you don't respond to them the way they think you should, then they don't think you love them. Once a person experiences rejection, he will find rejection even where it does not exist. I have even seen people who expect to be rejected. Satan will make sure they get what they expect.

Those who internalize their rejected feelings are not interpreting life properly. Stop the malfunction and stay out of the caves of depression and indifference. Don't disappear from the radar screen of life by running from God and those who love you. When rejection goes off (internalization), run to God and don't isolate yourself.

ALL ABOARD
THE WOE-IS-ME EXPRESS

As a pastor I sometimes feel unfairly treated by those who suffer with rejection. Some make me feel like I am supposed to chase after them and make sure they are all right, their needs are met, and they are happy. I liken it to an emotional roller coaster that people want me to climb aboard. When I don't participate, they get mad at me. It's almost like a form of control. If you miss one opportunity to minister to them, then they demonstrate their displeasure and are gone. It seems that they put undue pressure and unrealistic expectations upon me by trying to transfer their burden onto me rather than onto the Lord. A minister can never board the Woe-Is-Me Express.

PAYBACK IS HELL

It's a proven thing that we will reap what we sow. Scripture says so, and it has been confirmed by thousands. Consider this divorced mother's testimony. For years her children thought that she loved God more than she loved them because she would seldom include them in her church activities. In their eyes, God was more important than they. Remember, Satan takes every opportunity to twist and pervert. One day when her children were grown and on their own, she expected them to visit her at her birthday celebration. She was so excited with the opportunity to gather her children together. However, to her surprise, the children never showed up. The next day a phone call came from her oldest son. After asking him why he failed to show for the birthday celebration the son responded, "We were just paying you back for the times when you went to church instead of being with us." The mother told me, "Payback is hell." We must never allow Satan to use the weapon of rejection to separate us from God and our children.

LOVE, WHAT'S THAT?

One of the most common traits of rejection is the inability to feel loved. Because those suffering the pains of rejection build internal walls to keep from getting hurt, these same walls keep love from getting through. The rejected feel unworthy and think that God and others view them as unworthy too. They view God's promises for everyone else, but not for them. They ask themselves, "How could God love me when I don't even love myself?"

When we pray for the rejected we need to verbally tear down those walls that rejection has built and declare them worthy! These same walls make others think that they are unworthy, and don't deserve to be loved as they perceive themselves in the miserable condition that rejection created.

The good news is that, "God *is* love" and He wants to love you. He wants you to jump into his lap. He wants to wrap his arms around you and give you a big squeeze. He wants you to know that he is there for you. The word says, "This is what real love is: It is not our love for God; it is God's love for us in sending his Son to take away our sins" (1 John 4:10 NCV). God has already begun demonstrating his love for us by sending his Son. He will finish what he has started. Jesus promised that he would not "leave us nor forsake us" (Hebrews 13:5).

DON'T HELP ME I'M DROWNING

The rejected would rather drown in self-pity than ask for help. Consider Henry who does every thing he can to gain the acceptance of his fellow workers. He is always on time and never leaves work early. If there is anything that needs to be done, Henry is the first to step forward and volunteer.

Henry sounds like the perfect employee, doesn't he? Except Henry has one major problem. Because of rejection, Henry can't say 'No' when asked to do something. The results are very serious because Henry gets piled up and backlogged with so many things to do that he is driven into depression. He works himself to death. Not only that, but Henry would rather drown than ask for help. Why? Because those with rejection think that asking for help is a sign of weakness. Henry looks for acceptance in what he does. This makes him a performance-orientated worker. After a few months at Henry's new job, he enters the 'never-say-no' and 'never-ask-for-help' routine, thereby finding himself unable to perform. Since he is performance-orientated and will not ask for help he will set himself up to fail. Now Henry is looked upon by those at work as unfaithful, unable to keep his word, and unable to perform his duties. Soon people avoid associating with him, his employer dismisses him and rejection completes its assignment.

REJECTION FLASHBACKS

Sometimes things happen that will trigger a memory of a painful event from our past. One young lady told me that every time she heard a particular song on the radio it brought back memories of being rejected by her boyfriend. Every time she heard the song, she had to deal with the pain again. I call this a rejection flashback.

The devil doesn't do anything new. What worked on you before he will try again. If you get hit by a rejection flashback, take it captive with the word of God. Rejection flashbacks are trigger mechanisms of pain. Arrest and exchange those feelings with the word of God. Scripture says, "For though we walk in the flesh, we do not war after the flesh: {4} For the weapons of our warfare are not carnal, but mighty through God to the pulling down of strong holds. {5} Casting down imaginations, and every high thing that exalteth itself against the knowledge of God, and bringing into captivity every thought to the obedience of Christ" (2 Corinthians 10: 3-5 KJV).

OTHER REJECTION EXAMPLES

Dealing with feelings of rejection is not anything new. We can and will overcome! Other s have...

> Jesus was rejected, despised, unappreciated, acquainted with sorrows and grief (Isaiah 53:3, John 1:11, Matthew 8:34, 27:46). He is King of Kings and Lord of Lords.

> Noah was rejected for 120 years. Can you imagine building an ark (boat) when it had never even rained before? Noah turned away from the mockery of the people, obeyed God and kept on building (Genesis 7).

> Job's wife rejected him when she said, "Curse God and die" (Job 2:9). His friends also rejected him, but he forgave and God blessed him mightily (Job 19:19).

134

Joseph was rejected by his brothers and sold into slavery (Genesis 37:4). Even in the pit of abandonment, he held fast to his dream. Joseph became second only to Pharaoh in Egypt.

John the Baptist suffered from ministerial rejection by the religious leaders of Israel, but his voice made a way for Jesus even in the wilderness (Matthew 11:18).

Elijah felt the pains of rejection when he declared, "I'm the only one left" (1 Kings 19:14). Soon a chariot of fire escorted him to heaven.

UNDOING REJECTION

It is possible to undo what rejection has done by taking responsibility for your own actions and acknowledging your feelings. Share what is bothering you with Jesus and your pastor. Rejection's house is built by...

habit

learned behaviors

thought processes

assumptions

negative internalized feelings.

The way we respond to our emotions must change. We must learn to put others first, be generous and challenge those feelings of rejection. We don't want to relieve the symptoms of rejection, but we want to change our very core beliefs with the word of God. We must value correction, and set goals for improving our communication skills, and develope our ability to express ourselves. By following these examples one can learn to enjoy life. So in a nutshell the rejected must...

identify the source of rejection and the accompanying feelings.

seek deliverance from hurts, wounds, and pain (Luke 4:18).

reaffirm your accepted position in Christ (Ephesians 2:6).

cast all your cares on Jesus and tell Him exactly what you are feeling (1 Peter 5:7).

renew (renovate) your mind with truth (Romans 12:2).

forgive those who have hurt you (Matthew 6:12-15).

tear down the old personality that rejection built.

learn new communication and people skills.

accept correction as a valuable asset (Hebrews 12).

refuse to take things personally by internalizing negative feelings.

follow David's example by turning away, stating your cause and prophesying your future.

SUMMARY
UNDOING REJECTION

Even though the use of drugs, alcohol and other substances provide a short-term relief from pain, they eventually do severe damage by enabling destructive patterns, thus making the pain worse.

Those suffering from rejection are notorious for disappearing from sight.

A minister can never board the Woe-Is-Me Express.

One of the most common traits of rejection is the inability to feel loved.

The rejected feel unworthy and think that God and others view them as unworthy too.

The rejected view God's promises for everyone else but not for them.

The rejected are performance-orientated workers who look for acceptance in what they do.

Rejection flashbacks are trigger mechanisms of pain.

REFERENCE DEFINITIONS

The following is a short list of word definitions used in this book.

ADULLAM, CAVE OF
Cave of justice.

ARMOR BEARER
Hebrew *nasa,* to lift up, support, sustain, aid, and assist.

CAST
Hebrew *shalak* meaning to throw, hurl, fling, shed, cast off.

CHASTENING
Greek word *paidiuo* meaning to train, instruct, cause to learn, mold, and correct.

DECEIVE
The Greek word *paralogizomai* meaning to reckon wrong, cheat yourself, have a false reasoning, delude, circumvent.

DECEPTION
A condition caused by refusing to walk out (obey) the word of God.

DESPISE
Hebrew *bazah,* meaning to view as worthless.

FORGIVENESS
A choice we make through the use of our wills.

FORSAKEN
Hebrew word *azab* meaning to depart, leave, desert, forsake, neglect, and abandon.

IDENTIFICATION
To put oneself in another's place, understand and share the thoughts, feelings, emotions, and problems of another.

ITERNALIZE
To take rejection personally by making it your own.

JEALOUS
Very watchful, resentfully suspicious, and envious.

TAKE
Hebrew *laqach* means to lay-hold of, seize, carry away, procure to himself, capture, remove.

MATURE
To be fully developed, aged, completed.

RECONCILIATION
When *two* people who have separated because of a disagreement come back together.

REJECTION
The feeling of not being liked, accepted, loved, valued, or received. It is the state of feeling unwanted, unaccepted, or unappreciated.

SUSTAIN
Hebrew *kuwl* meaning to hold-up, nourish, refresh, support and supply.

SNARE
Hebrew *mowqesh,* meaning bait, lure, or trap.

SOUL
The mind, will, intellect, reasoning, imaginations and emotions.

SYMPATHY
The Greek expression for "touched with the feeling" is *sumpatheo* meaning to have compassion, be affected with the same feeling as another, sympathize with, feel for, and identify with. From the Greek word *sumpatheo* we get our English word sympathy.

TRANSFORMED
The Greek word *metamorphoo* meaning to be changed into another form. This teaches us that the word of God, when used to renovate our minds, will gradually morph us into the proper personality.

SCRIPTURE REFERENCES

"For ye are dead, and your life is hid with Christ in God. {4} When Christ, who is our life, shall appear, then shall ye also appear with him in glory. {5} Mortify therefore your members which are upon the earth; fornication, uncleanness, inordinate affection, evil concupiscence, and covetousness, which is idolatry: {6} For which things' sake the wrath of God cometh on the children of disobedience: {7} In the which ye also walked some time, when ye lived in them. {8} But now ye also put off all these; anger, wrath, malice, blasphemy, filthy communication out of your mouth. {9} Lie not one to another, seeing that ye have put off the old man with his deeds; {10} And have put on the new man, which is renewed in knowledge after the image of him that created him: {11} Where there is neither Greek nor Jew, circumcision nor uncircumcision, Barbarian, Scythian, bond nor free: but Christ is all, and in all. {12} Put on therefore, as the elect of God, holy and beloved, bowels of mercies, kindness, humbleness of mind, meekness, longsuffering; {13} Forbearing one another, and forgiving one another, if any man have a quarrel against any: even as Christ forgave you, so also do ye. {14} And above all these things put on charity, which is the bond of perfectness. {15} And let the peace of God rule in your hearts, to the which also ye are called in one body; and be ye thankful." (Colossians 3:3-15 KJV)

"Wherefore, my beloved, as ye have always obeyed, not as in my presence only, but now much more in my absence, work out your own salvation with fear and trembling." (Philippians 2:12 KJV)

"Not as though I had already attained, either were already perfect: but I follow after, if that I may apprehend that for which also I am apprehended of Christ Jesus." (Philippians 3:12 KJV)

"Wherefore laying aside all malice, and all guile, and hypocrisies, and envies, and all evil speakings, {2} As newborn babes, desire the sincere milk of the word, that ye may grow thereby: {3} If so be ye have tasted that the Lord is gracious." (1 Peter 2:1-3 KJV)

"Let the word of Christ dwell in you richly in all wisdom; teaching and admonishing one another in psalms and hymns and spiritual songs, singing with grace in your hearts to the Lord." (Colossians 3:16 KJV)

"For the word of God is quick, and powerful, and sharper than any two-edged sword, piercing even to the dividing asunder of soul and spirit, and of the joints and marrow, and is a discerner of the thoughts and intents of the heart." (Hebrews 4:12 KJV)

"I die daily." (1 Corinthians 15:31 KJV)

"For which cause we faint not; but though our outward man perish, yet the inward man is renewed day by day." (2 Corinthians 4:16 KJV)

"Casting down imaginations, and every high thing that exalteth itself against the knowledge of God, and bringing into captivity every thought to the obedience of Christ." (2 Corinthians 10:5 KJV)

"But we all, with open face beholding as in a glass the glory of the Lord, are changed into the same image from glory to glory, even as by the Spirit of the Lord." (2 Corinthians 3:18 KJV)

"Wherefore he is able also to save them to the uttermost that come unto God by him, seeing he ever liveth to make intercession for them." (Hebrews 7:25 KJV)

"Being confident of this very thing, that he which hath begun a good work in you will perform it until the day of Jesus Christ:" (Philippians 1:6 KJV)

"But he answered and said, Every plant, which my heavenly Father hath not planted, shall be rooted up." (Matthew 15:13 KJV)

"For a good tree bringeth not forth corrupt fruit; neither doth a corrupt tree bring forth good fruit. {44} For every tree is known by his own fruit. For of thorns men do not gather figs, nor of a bramble bush gather they grapes. {45} A good man out of the good treasure of his heart bringeth forth that which is good; and an evil man out of the evil treasure of his heart bringeth forth that which is evil: for of the abundance of the heart his mouth speaketh." (Luke 6:43-45 KJV)

"And why call ye me, Lord, Lord, and do not the things which I say? {47} Whosoever cometh to me, and heareth my sayings, and doeth them, I will show you to whom he is like: {48} He is like a man which built an house, and digged deep, and laid the foundation on a rock: and when the flood arose, the stream beat vehemently upon that house, and could not shake it: for it was founded upon a rock. {49} But he that heareth, and doeth not, is like a man that without a foundation built an house upon the earth; against which the stream did beat vehemently, and immediately it fell; and the ruin of that house was great." (Luke 6:46-49 KJV)

"And he said to them all, If any man will come after me, let him deny himself, and take up his cross daily, and follow me. {24} For whosoever will save his life shall lose it: but whosoever will lose his life for my sake, the same shall save it." (Luke 9:23-24 KJV)

"A new heart also will I give you, and a new spirit will I put within you: and I will take away the stony heart out of your flesh, and I will give you an heart of flesh. {27} And I will put my spirit within you, and cause you to walk in my statutes, and ye shall keep my judgments, and do them." (Ezekiel 36:26-27 KJV)

"The spirit of the Lord GOD is upon me; because the LORD hath anointed me to preach good tidings unto the meek; he hath sent me to bind up the broken-hearted, to proclaim liberty to the captives, and the opening of the prison to them that are bound; {2} To proclaim the acceptable year of the LORD, and the day of vengeance of our God; to comfort all that mourn; {3} To appoint unto them that mourn in Zion, to give unto them beauty for ashes, the oil of joy for mourning, the garment of praise for the spirit of heaviness; that they might be called trees of righteousness, the planting of the LORD, that he might be glorified." (Isaiah 61:1-3 KJV)

"Every branch in me that beareth not fruit he taketh away: and every branch that beareth fruit, he purgeth it, that it may bring forth more fruit." (John 15:2 KJV)

"But speaking the truth in love, may grow up into him in all things, which is the head, even Christ:" (Ephesians 4:15 KJV)

INDEX

A

Abandoned Tamar 60
Abandonment 5, 17, 27, 28, 59, 75, 76, 80, 103, 131
Abilities 92
Ability to forgive 110
Ability to mature 89
Abinadab 35, 42
Abnormally anxious 18
Absalom 34, 55, 57, 60, 62, 64, 65, 76
Absalom lied 66
Absalom's treachery 68
Abuse 5, 17, 119
Acceptance 5, 84
Accepted 4, 16
Accepted in the beloved 86
Accepted with him 84
Addictions 123
Afraid of God 21
Agreeable 117
Ahab 30, 120
Ahithophel 76
Air traffic controllers 124
Airspace 124
Alcohol 123
Amnon 55, 57, 58, 59
Anguish 76
Anxiety 104
Appearance 19
Appreciated 4
Appreciation 124
Arrogance 67

Ascension gifts 27, 90
Assumptions 132
Attacks against value 89
Attitude 124
Author and finisher 102
Auto-pilot 124
Aviation 124
Azab 28

B

Baalhazor 61
Balaam 30
Bankruptcy 17
Baptism in the Holy Spirit 109
Basic need 16
Bathsheba 76
Bazah 50
Begin the healing 22
Bethlehem 35
Betrayal 5, 75, 76, 80
Bitterness 21, 65, 67, 104, 107, 109
Blueprints 10
Books 19
Bore our sicknesses 79
Bridge of communication 100
Bringing into captivity 130

C

Capture 30
Cast 79
Casting down imaginations 129
Cause to learn 93
Causes of rejection 16
Caves of depression 125
Champion of Israel 33
Change your mind 95

147

151

INVITATION

Hello friends and partners!

In addition to preaching the gospel around the world, we also have a powerful church in South Florida and would love to have you visit with us. The Spirit of God told us to start a church and raise up people in strength and power who would reach their city and impact the nations. SOLM has an international apostolic and prophetic call, as well as a mandate to raise up a strong local church by ministering to the whole family. SOLM has the reputation of being a place where you can receive what you need from the Lord; whether it be healing, miracles, deliverance, restoration, victory, or success. Why? Because with God all things are possible. SOLM' uniqueness is being recognized and sought after as we continue growing in spiritual liberty, influence, strength and power. We invite you to come and receive confirmation, impartation, and activation.

In the Master's service,
Jonas and Rhonda Clark

JEZEBEL SEDUCING GODDESS OF WAR

Jezebel is the warrior goddess who has gone unchallenged in our generation. Dr. Lester Sumrall said that she would be the greatest opposer of the apostolic church before the coming of the Lord. In 1933 Voice of Healing Prophet William Branham had a vision of her rising to take control.

"Some people write about things that they know nothing about. Not this time! It is time to barbecue this spirit."

ISBN 1-886885-04-4

50 EARMARKS OF AN APOSTOLIC CHURCH

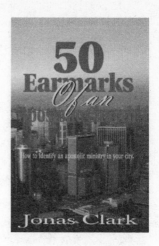

Jesus said, "I will build my church and the gates of hell shall not prevail." So what kind of church is it that Jesus is building? Is it a religious church? A traditional church? A defeated church? Or is it a glorious church without spot or wrinkle?

Right now we are experiencing an awesome paradigm shift in ministry. The Holy Spirit is moving us into a time of the restoration of the apostolic ministry. All over the world God is birthing apostolic churches. But what do they look like? What makes them so different? Is there one in your city? In this thought-provoking book Jonas teaches you 50 earmarks of an apostolic church in your city. It's time to cross the bridge into the apostolic. Are you ready to be a part of an exciting glorious church?

ISBN 1-886885-06-0

PROPHETIC OPERATIONS

The prophets may give personal prophecies, but their revelation gifting goes way beyond personal prophecy. Power, money, prestige, honor, promotion, and enticements, with smooth flattering sayings, are all demonic assignments designed to pull on any common ground that might be in the heart of God's prophetic ministers.

Our society is filled with those who come into our churches who have formerly opened themselves up to new age mysticism, witchcraft, the occult, and spiritualism. To protect the flock from false anointings and familiar spirits, there is a proper order in which the Holy Spirit likes to flow.

It's time for accurate prophetic operations!

ISBN 1-886885-11-7

EXPOSING SPIRITUAL WITCHCRAFT

Spiritual witchcraft is the power of Satan. Its purpose is to control and manipulate you.

The weapons of witchcraft are emotional manipulation, spiritual and religious control, isolation, soul ties, fear, confusion, loss of personal identity, sickness, depression and prophetic divination.

Those caught in the snare of this spirit struggle all their Christian life to remain stable in their walk with Christ.

Topics include: the character of spiritual witchcraft, the weapons of witchcraft, the road to deception and lastly — breaking free!

"I fought this spirit from April to November and won. So can you!"

ISBN 1-886885-00-1

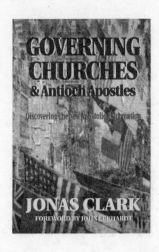

GOVERNING CHURCHES & ANTIOCH APOSTLES

Apostolic churches build, guide, govern, blast, establish, carry liberty, impart blessing, set, father, mature, set the pace, influence, train, send, launch, hear, say and do.

A new move of the Holy Spirit has begun! It is the call for a new apostolic reformation. This reformation is challenging old religious structures and systems. It is restoring the understanding of an apostolic church that will enable us to fulfill the great commission. It's time to discover your role in the new apostolic reformation.

ISBN 1-886885-07-9

IMAGINATIONS DON'T LIVE THERE!

Have you floated out into an imagination today? The Word of God teaches us to be led by the Spirit of God. However, we must first learn how to conquer the weird world of soulish imaginations. An imagination is a picture conceived in the spirit of one's mind that forms a mental picture of what is not. Imaginations speak of things that haven't happened and are not real. Once spoken they come alive. When acted on they lead to fear, instability, and feelings of insecurity. The freedom to imagine must first be fortified with truth. This book will help you take control of your mind and free you to be led by the Spirit of God.

ISBN 1-886885-03-6

COME OUT!

It is time for the church
to exercise her author-
ity against Satan who
has been allowed to
maintain his oppres-
sion without a chal-
lenge. In this handbook
for the serious deliver-
ance minister we will
study...

the scriptural foundations for deliverance

how to continue the deliverance ministry of
Jesus

the different types of spirits mentioned in
the Bible

how to cast out devils

six things evil spirits attach themselves to

how to keep our deliverance

and much more.

ISBN 1-886885-10-0

RELIGIOUS SPIRITS

One of the most deadly influences in the body of Christ today is the religious spirit.

Religious people themselves have been used as the devil's assassins, targeting the spiritually young, the zealous, the hungry and the leadership.

This book will speak into the lives of those who are being spiritually abused by religious spirits who steal the spiritual zeal from God-called, anointed, and appointed children of God.

All of us have experienced the onslaught of the religious spirit in our lives. This book will open the eyes of those who themselves have been seduced into religious forms and traditions of men, and offer them a way out of carnal religious activity.

ISBN 1-886885-12-5

Global Cause Network

THE GLOBAL CAUSE NETWORK is a network of churches and ministries that have united together to build a platform for an apostolic voice. The *GCN* is built on relationships rather than denominational politics. It consists of those who recognize the importance of apostolic gifts working together with all five ascension gifts to equip believers for the work of ministry. By uniting we have forged an alliance across the globe that is building a 'great net for a great catch.' The foundational vision of the *GCN* is covenant relationships between its membership for the advancement of the gospel of Jesus Christ throughout the world.

MISSION STATEMENT

• To reach the world with the gospel of Jesus Christ.

• To build and strengthen the local church.

THE GLOBAL CAUSE NETWORK PROVIDES...

• apostolic and prophetic identity with a strong sense of community

• a platform to coordinate, enhance and re-lease God's apostolic and prophetic voice

• a focus to impact our cities and the nations with the gospel

• apostolic covering, confirmation, impartation, activation, team ministry, sending, church planting and release of ministry gifts

• critical learning resources, educational and informational materials vital to the advancement of the network

• apostolic fathering, focus and direction

• facilitation of relationship by connecting those of like precious faith together

For more information contact the GCN ministry office.

The Global Cause Network
Apostle Jonas Clark
27 West Hallandale Beach Blvd
Hallandale, Florida
33009
(954) 456-4420

email: life@catchlife.org
Web site www.catchlife.org

MINISTRY INFORMATION

For a complete ministry catalog of tapes, books and videos, or to invite Jonas to speak at your next conference, please contact

Spirit of Life Ministries
27 West Hallandale Beach Blvd.
Hallandale, Florida 33009
(954) 456-4420

email: life@catchlife.org

BOOKS
BY JONAS CLARK

Jezebel, Seducing Goddess of War

Exposing Spiritual Witchcraft

Apostolic Equipping Dimension

Come Out!

Governing Churches & Antioch Apostles

50 Earmarks of an Apostolic Church

Imaginations, Don't Live There!

Prophetic Operations

Religious Spirits

Available in
quality Christian bookstores or
easy on-line internet ordering
http://catchlife.org or call toll free
(800) 943-6490

Spirit of Life Ministries
27 West Hallandale Beach Blvd.
Hallandale, Florida 33009
(954) 456-4420

email: life@catchlife.org